Better Mondays

The New Rules for Creating Financial Success and Personal Freedom (While Working for the Man)

By

Roger A. Reid

Better Mondays: The New Rules for Creating Financial Success and Personal Freedom (While Working for the Man)

Copyright © 2020 by Roger A. Reid

Redstone Press

ISBN 978-1-7358607-0-1

Printed in the United States of America

www.RogerReid.com

Table of Contents

Notes from the Author

Notes from the Author
Is this book for you?

I wrote this book for a specific audience—a select group that is ready to utilize the advantages of the corporation to achieve financial success and personal satisfaction with their career. You may already be a part of this elite tribe. If so, you know that in nearly every way that counts, you're very much like other motivated, successful employees—*but with one major difference* . . .

It's Your Life First.

While you project every indication of being a dedicated company man or woman on the outside, you're in the game for yourself. Your decisions are made from the standpoint of what serves you best—in both the short and long-term. Your ongoing relationship with your employer is based on what the company can do for you, and how much you'll ultimately derive from working there.

Better Mondays will help you . . .

- Accomplish your financial goals while meeting your company's expectations

- Use your job as a stepping stone to create the career you really want

- Become known as an "Expert" within your industry

- Find meaning, fulfillment, and a sense of satisfaction from your work

Yes, on occasion, you've no doubt felt the lure of striking out on your own. You may have even considered the possibility of starting your own business, enjoying the occasional daydream about shedding the layers of bureaucracy, cronyism, politics, and the day-to-day bullshit associated with big business.

But you've also realized the truth: Anytime you deal with other people's needs and wants, you're going to have to deal with bullshit. It's the result of trying to meet the subjective, unrealistic, and sometimes, the unreasonable expectations of others, and it happens *whether you are an employee or an entrepreneur.*

It's a simple point, but a vital one: There is little difference between an employee and an entrepreneur when examined under the conceptual light of exchanging service for compensation. It all comes down to one inescapable fact: The very concept of work is based on serving the needs of others. An entrepreneur serves his or her customers. An employee serves the company directives.

The Sources of the Information Contained in This Book

Before you dive into the main part of the book, I'd like to provide some insight into the source of this information and why I believe it's valid.

First, I was adamant this book would not be a rehashing of past sociological studies or a review of psychological data presented as a thematic collection of references to substantiate a specific premise.

To avoid this "derivative effect," I decided the material had to be originally sourced, either from my own experiences or from that of others who agreed to share them.

Second, I insisted the content be applicable, not only in today's constant debate between the advantages and drawbacks of a corporate career versus the entrepreneurial alternative but within the corporation itself, to give the reader an edge in influencing their longevity and success with their employer.

I'll admit that before I began my first edit, I was concerned about the "usability" qualifier being too subjective. Knowing that each reader would approach the material with a different level of career experience made me even less sure where to draw the line on what to include and what to leave out. However, as I began receiving feedback from my group of beta test readers, the relevant material became obvious.

If the information helped explain, illustrated a point, or offered specific insights about real-world situations, it made the cut. If it drifted off-topic or gave voice to an irrelevant or dissenting opinion merely for argument's sake, I cut it. (I'm also pointing my finger at myself here, as I found I was as much a violator as any of my other sources.)

Throughout the book, I refer to "Acme" Corporation. It's a synonym for the Fortune 500 company where I was employed for fourteen years. The events and situations described are presented as learning experiences.

Finally, I want you to know that I've approached this project in the most realistic fashion possible. I've tried to identify the vital components of finding financial success within a corporate environment while experiencing the satisfaction of doing meaningful work. I've also placed a few red flags when and where appropriate. I realize this transparent approach to revealing the internal workings of the typical corporate employer-employee relationship won't make many points with Human Resources, and that's fine. They don't need to read this book; they already know their ultimate purpose.

As you read, I encourage you to ask a question or two and then determine what's true for you. My goals in writing this book are simple and straightforward: To help you build a financially rewarding career, take pride in your professional and personal accomplishments, and derive a long-term sense of satisfaction from how you choose to spend the working years of your life.

Chapter One
Let's Get Real

Let's start with a question:

With all the current emphasis on entrepreneurship as the preferred career choice, why would anyone write a book about creating a successful and rewarding career by working for someone else—and not just anyone else, but a large corporation, with its inherent politics, hidden agendas, and adherence to the herd mentality? It's just the opposite of the popular career rhetoric that preaches self-employment as the ideal way to wealth, independence, and happiness.

It's no secret that with a majority of business authors, bloggers, and career strategists touting the advantages of being an entrepreneur, bashing the corporation has become trendy and fashionable. And moving away from the supposed drudgery and unrewarding routine of working for the man is the popular fantasy.

However, for most Americans, that's exactly what it remains—a fantasy.

While business ownership may be the dream, here are the facts:

The overwhelming majority of the American workforce are employees. They work for someone. That "someone" might be a Fortune 500 Hundred company employing thousands of people, or a small business with just a few employees on the payroll.

It's hard to understate the importance of these numbers. They tell us that most of the working population is *not* in business for themselves. They work in and for the business of others, adhering to company policy, procedures, and methods that usually pre-existed their hiring.

The numbers also tell us something even more important: The overwhelming majority of people are satisfied—even happy—with a conventional eight-to-five job, *even when they say they are not.*

Yes, a large percentage of employees complain about their job, but they seldom consider their grievances sufficiently motivating to relinquish the advantages provided by their employer. Although they may argue they would much rather be in charge of their professional destiny, their complaints usually reflect temporary disappointments and dissatisfaction inherent in *any* occupation.

In short, they're comfortable with the relationship they have with the boss and consider the inherent company bureaucracy a necessary and inescapable part of working for the man—in effect, a reasonable tradeoff for the benefit of relatively consistent work, and the opportunity to build long-term financial security. It's these genuine advantages that continue to drive new college grads to large corporations and motivates job changing executives to stay on a corporate career path.

So before we go any further, let's get something straight . . . *Not everyone wants to be an entrepreneur!*

(Gasp!) That's right. I said it. And I said it because it's true. More about that later, but first, let's look at the main reasons so many still choose to work for the man.

Immediate and consistent income. Working for a business powerhouse, with its inherent financial reserves and assets, means there's less chance of suffering a loss of income in the event of a temporary market reversal, or even a general economic downturn. You may have to do a little creative self-marketing to substantiate your value, but a large, economically sound corporation is a good place to weather the ups and downs of the marketplace that have become commonplace in our continually changing economic picture.

You acquire immediate credibility. Belonging to a well-funded, productive, and recognized force in your chosen field grants you immediate credibility. For many, working for a corporation satisfies a need to be a part of something larger than themselves. They find satisfaction in having a large part of their identity defined by their association with their employer, especially when others recognize them as an integral and important member of a successful organization.

For many professions, it's the right—if not the only—"fit." For example, technical people, engineers, researchers, planners, scientists, computer programmers, and other "analytical types," typically find the working environment in a large company to be exactly what they need. In many cases, these workers are intelligent—some are brilliant—well-adjusted, hard-working individuals who are happiest when they can concentrate on assigned tasks with pre-defined parameters, and do it without having to be concerned about all the details of running their own company. They have no desire to worry about company taxes, balancing the budget, or profit margins—unless that's their area of responsibility.

It's a place to grow and prove yourself. Having an existing organizational structure to negotiate, climb, and eventually conquer, appeals to those born with a management personality, who see the corporation as a place to be tamed and mastered. They're typically competitive, politically savvy fast-trackers who have their eye on a vice-presidency, access to the company jet, and want to see their picture in the annual report. They go where and when the company tells them, collecting promotions and raises along the way. Often valuing titles more than compensation, they love to chat about internalizing profit centers through divisionalization and departmental micro-managing. They usually represent the very essence of a "company man," and their loyalty cannot be questioned—until they are pirated away by the competition (a useful career strategy we'll talk about later).

Investment benefits. This includes access to 401K plans, privileged stock purchases, health insurance, and other "group" discounted advantages. Investing in the company you work for provides the benefit of an in-depth understanding of what you're buying and how it compares to the competition. You know the industry and you understand your company's operation within it, giving you far more insight than is contained in a stock analyst's projections and recommendation.

The above five benefits only scratch the surface, especially when we consider the value of the relationships we build with co-workers, management, customers, and yes, even the competition.

Each individual has a different idea of what's important when evaluating a career choice. While some have their priority on compensation, others want a flexible work environment. Still, others need some degree of independence and autonomy. The list can also include things like recognition, status, travel, access to proprietary systems and tools, and the association with other technologically-minded or industry-specific individuals—benefits that are often only available under the roof of a large organization.

In short, a large corporation provides a defined structure—complete with processes and procedures—in which to create, process, and deliver value. And there are plenty of people who thrive on this kind of organizational discipline, accomplishing their best work under the corporate umbrella while finding a sense of satisfaction in what they do for a living.

Yes, the dream of running your own business empire is a compelling thought, but just as there are those who aspire to own their own business and can't wait to gain their financial independence, there are many more who are born to follow, to fit in, to find a place where they can contribute.

Things Have Changed . . . Forty years ago, "working for the man" meant a job for life, identity by association, and confirmation of personal value, evidenced by a monthly paycheck. In the most literal sense, the purpose of "working for a living" was to generate money—to buy food, pay for housing, buy a car and take a two-week vacation once a year. The other (subjective) metrics of a satisfying career didn't matter. It was a simple mantra: Show up on time, put in the hours, go home, repeat for thirty years.

Today, deriving a sense of meaning and purpose from your work often competes in equal priority with compensation, time-work life balance, geographic location, and a positive, supportive work environment.

With the amount of opportunity in today's job market, no one should be at the mercy of a draconian employer. Working within a corporate environment shouldn't mean you have to give away your dignity and self-respect. And it certainly doesn't mean conforming to the hive mentality and slaving away at some mindless job like a worker-drone.

Yes, things have changed—on both sides of the career equation. Choosing a corporate career can be a managed path to financial freedom while deriving satisfaction from your work.

My goal is to help you make the most of your relationship with your employer—to maximize the advantages and benefits while reducing your exposure to the negative aspects inherent in any large organization.

If you only take one thing away from this book, I hope it's this: The relationship you have with your employer can be *managed*. And knowing the nature of the beast will give you a tremendous advantage in making day-to-day work decisions as well as long-term career choices.

The bottom line? If the majority of us are working for an employer, why not determine the best way to manage that relationship? You have the opportunity to make the most of your current career situation—right now! And once you learn how to influence and manage the vital relationships that influence career success, you may find the advantages of working for the man far outweigh the drawbacks.

Read on!

Chapter Two
Choose Wisely

You've just received an offer! You're excited. And you should be. It's an opportunity that could change your life.

The question is, will the change be for the better . . . or worse? If you accept the offer, will you look back on the decision as a good one? Or will you regret it, wishing you had known more about what you were getting yourself into?

Remember, we're talking about making a commitment to being present—mentally and physically—for the majority of your waking hours. And when you're not actually on the job, you'll be thinking about your work or getting ready to go to work, or spending time commuting. Essentially, you'll be arranging the rest of your life around your job.

"Okay, it's a big deal. I get that. Now what?"

Unless the offer is specifically time-bound with a short window for acceptance, send a letter of appreciation to the company. Then take the next couple of days to research and evaluate the company as a prospective employer.

The process of vetting any large company is easier if organized into two parts: Basic and Internal. Basic information includes company history, number of employees, locations of headquarters, regional offices and branches, as well as manufacturing facilities, if any. You also need to know what products or services they sell, and if possible, their relative or comparative priority, based on the amount of profit they generate. This may sound difficult, but you'll be surprised at what you can find online.

Why the third degree? If you're being hired to work for the division that makes blue gizmos, but blue gizmos is a loss leader, and a year later, the company drops blue gizmos from the product line, your job may be in limbo.

You should also determine if the company's products are designed and assembled in-house (high-profit margins with a substantial company investment in infrastructure), or purchased from another manufacturer (profit primarily generated from mark-up and value-added, without primary control over manufacturing costs or availability).

The first situation is typically more stable and creates the bread and butter of any large company's profit picture. The second means the company's revenues are dependent upon a third party, which can put your job in jeopardy if the company-to-company relationship changes.

If you're a skilled job hunter, most of these research questions probably seem obvious. However, you'd be amazed by the number of people who readily admit they accepted their current job because "it was offered to me." In retrospect, they often wish they had done more due diligence before signing on.

Let's go into more detail about the basics. Here's what you need to know *as a minimum:*

1.   Have a clear and concise description of the work. If the job description is vague or full of non-specific, industry buzz-words, you may need to ask for the three (or five, or?) most important daily functions for which you'll be responsible.

2.   Are there activities you'll be expected to perform not mentioned in the job description? This might include running to the office supply store, setting up trade show displays, making a daily trip to the post office, or delivering samples to customers.

3.   How will your performance be evaluated? Are there specific parameters or metrics? How often will you and your work be reviewed?

4. If the position is an hourly compensated job, confirm the work hours and the length of lunch and coffee breaks. If the company asks you to stay late or work half a day on Saturday, will you receive compensation, either in the form of additional income or time-credit?

5. Should you expect regular contact (text, phone, or email) about work issues after-hours or on the weekends? If your weekends are going to be interrupted by questions from your boss, you need to know that upfront.

6. If the position is salaried, ask what hours the other employees typically arrive and leave the office, and how many hours are usually required on the weekends to stay even with the workload and meet the expectations of management.

7. How much travel is involved, including the number of overnights per month?

8. If any part of your compensation is based on a bonus or commission, are you eligible to participate from your first day on the job? Or is there a waiting or intern period in which bonus participation is waived or reduced?

9. What's included in the benefits package? Calculate the value of health insurance, 401K plans, stock options, use of a company car, vacation days, and retirement benefits when comparing offers.

10. If the commute is lengthy, ask if the office location is fixed for the foreseeable future. If there are plans to move it, ask about alternative locations under consideration to determine if the new commute will be closer or further from your home.

11. This is your catch-all question, covering everything from typical or expected dress, to the actual work environment (cubical, shared office, private space?).

Based on the information you gather, determine if you can answer the "Big Four." These questions represent the four main reasons employees eventually leave their employer for greener pastures. If you see any of these situations as possible problems in the future, bring up your concerns with the hiring manager and be specific—it's your future, and if you perceive possible conflicts in policy, work-life balance, the opportunity for advancement or compensation, addressing it now could save you lots of time and frustration a year or two down the road.

1. Will you have autonomy in your work? Or will the boss be breathing down your neck, checking every step of your assignment? Most of us need the mental and physical space to do our job. We also want the opportunity to exercise our responsibility and be acknowledged for doing it correctly. A boss who is constantly correcting, re-directing, or flooding you with suggestions on "how he would do it," will have you looking for another job in the short term.

2. Are there opportunities for more responsibility and compensation as you grow in capability? Or does your job description give you the impression of being locked in, unable to move beyond the function for which you were initially hired? If you're planning on earning the highest levels of income your profession provides, you're going to have to move up in status, position, or title—regardless of "blue sky" promises of compensation based solely on productivity. The general rule for most organizations is that bosses make more money than subordinates. It's a part of the bureaucratic system, and exceptions are rare.

For example, when I went to work for Acme, I noticed a common situation—sales engineers remaining in that same position for over twenty years. I was told it was a personal choice, and it wasn't unusual for a sales engineer to stay at that job level for their entire career. I was also told their contribution was so important to the overall success of the company that their compensation was not limited by job function or title, and the best performers could expect to make the same income as a regional manager—two managerial positions above sales engineer. The promise turned out to be a motivational lie. In my fourteen years with the company, I never personally knew of any sales engineer making close to a regional manager's income. In fact, when my productivity began to generate levels of compensation equal to that of a regional manager, the sales credit I'd accumulated began "disappearing" off my quarterly performance reports (more about that later.)

3. Do the company's expectations seem out of balance, requiring you to give up high priority personal activities such as time with family? If so, ask yourself how long before you resent the company's intrusion on your personal life.

4. How do you feel about the *current* compensation package you're being offered? Is it enough to give you a sense of being rewarded for your commitment and exchange of time? Regardless of your personal priorities, money is one way to keep score. It's an indication of value. And it's damn important. Make sure you're starting salary is competitive within your industry. And as I mentioned before, don't overlook the importance of the benefit package. Health insurance, 401K plans, and other perks have real value. Always include them when determining the total bottom line.

Keep this in mind when evaluating an offer of compensation: If, after taking the job, you know you'll still have money worries, or will have to consider part-time employment to cover the bills, you need to rethink your career choice and maybe your entire financial picture. If you're overspending or living an unrealistic lifestyle, you can and should adjust your spending to match your income. However, if you're financially burdened with student loan payments, child support, medical bills, or other involuntary expense, you may need to talk to a financial advisor or an attorney.

Now let's change the focus of our evaluation to the internal workings of the company. This information is not going to be as apparent as the basics and in some cases, can be a bit more challenging to obtain. But it's what you must know before you can make an informed decision about committing to a prospective employer.

Very much like two sides of a mirror, every company has two images. One side—the one everyone can see—typically reflects a picture of evolving perfection. Usually highlighted by a positive work culture, it presents the company as an organization where everyone receives the support they need, the respect they deserve, and the assurance of a financially secure future.

Turn the mirror over, and the image can be very different. This view might include skeleton-filled closets and a Muzak system masking the conversations of executives nonchalantly discussing the fate of several hundred employees about to be discharged as the result of a company take-over or a division-wide layoff.

The point of this metaphor is to demonstrate that management's real goals may be very different from the image they project to the public. Don't be fooled into believing company rhetoric about living a balanced life or putting family first—unless there is hard evidence to prove it. Companies claiming to emphasize family culture, personally-directed career pathing, or a life-in-balance philosophy, typically flaunt these benefits as intrinsic and fundamental values of the organization. In reality, these "feel good" programs *must* serve a profit motivation. The moment they can no longer be measured as improvements to the bottom line or in employee retention, they'll be eliminated as costly and ineffective. (If this sounds counter-intuitive, there's more about corporate culture and how to evaluate psychic benefits in Chapter Seven.)

Your success will be determined by your immediate supervisor. There is no better predictor of your ultimate level of success than the quality of your relationship with your immediate supervisor. This includes not only the boss you'll interact with on a daily basis but also those who work at the highest levels of management, some of which you may never personally meet until you begin moving up through promotion.

These decision-makers generally fall into three groups: Your direct supervisor, middle and upper management, and the owners (if the company is privately owned). These are the people in charge, and they will ultimately determine your future, *regardless of the activities you perform on a day-to-day basis.*

Does this mean your daily job performance isn't essential to your career? No, it means your relationship with those in charge will have MORE to do with your success than your work accomplishments.

Don't believe it? If you've been on the job for several years, you've no doubt questioned some of the promotions given to co-workers because you knew the recipients were either unqualified or undeserving. Even if the lack of qualifications wasn't outright obvious, the circumstances surrounding the promotion were suspicious in merit. Conversely, how many dedicated employees can you name who did outstanding work, and yet were ignored, year after year?

If you're just starting your corporate career and have little to no experience dealing with organizational hierarchy, I'll assure you, the number on both sides of the fence—those who receive undeserved positions and those never recognized for outstanding work— is enough to justify the premise.

Examine the company's senior management. What kind of people are they? Conservative or innovative? Do they typically default to the status quo? Or do they readily adopt new technology, processes, and procedures?

If you can't personally meet with members of senior management, this may require a few calculated assumptions based on what you learn from the environment, your future manager, and other employees with whom you're able to speak. Start by researching each manager's history. Compare their career paths. Did they start their working career with the company, or were they hired from a previous employer? If they came from another company, was it one within the same industry, or from an unrelated field? In their previous position, were they credited with reversing negative situations or profits? What kind of legacy did they leave?

Once you have a sense of what drives senior management, ask yourself this: How does your personal goals, objectives, work ethic, personality, education, and experience compare to the ten most influential managers in the company? The top ten in any company represent the "model" manager—the type of person the board of directors and owners count on to make consistent and acceptable decisions year after year.

If you find that your mindset is so different from the mentality of the most visible company managers that the idea of sitting down with them to chat about your future relationship with the company makes you uncomfortable, you need to look elsewhere.

To familiarize yourself with the company's management style before accepting any job offer, use these four qualifying questions:

1.   How successful are the previous new hires that started at the same entry position, after three, five, and ten years?

2.   What does the company's growth history look like over the last five, ten, and twenty-year periods?

3. What are the short and long-term priorities of senior management (for example, to maximize profit, aggressive expansion, conservative growth, or to sell the company)?

4. Before accepting the position, will you be granted permission to speak privately with any of the employees, especially those working at the same job offered to you? Although there will always be employees who can find something wrong with their employer or express dissatisfaction with their work situation, the consensus of those you talk to should confirm a positive relationship with the company.

Plan on doing at least as much research about the company as they will do about you. For example, interviewers ask for references because they want third-party verification that you're honest, loyal, trustworthy, and have accomplished the achievements you've listed on your resume. For you to do the same is sensible and prudent.

If your preliminary examination is positive, ask the hiring manager if you could spend an hour in the office where you'll be working. A potential employer should interpret your request as a positive sign. It says you're interested in the job and you want to invest more time to make sure the future relationship between you and your employer will be a good one.

Bob Sutton, a Stanford Professor, organizational researcher, and best-selling author of *The No Asshole Rule* and *Good Boss, Bad Boss*, takes it even a step further. He advises his students to take a long and careful look at the people they're going to be working with because the odds are overwhelmingly in favor of you becoming like them, instead of them becoming like you.

As you evaluate your potential co-workers, keep in mind that most will be on their best behavior, so it may be difficult to come to any hard and fast conclusions. Do your best to draw them out with questions that can't be answered with a simple "yes" or "no." How do their values, beliefs, and priorities compare with yours? Can you imagine yourself "fitting in" with the majority of your future work-mates? If not, there's a good chance you're going to be miserable, and it's just a matter of time before you're looking for a way out.

If your request to visit with company employees is refused, or you're told you'll see the working environment *after* you're hired because it's against "policy," or your presence would be a disruption to the employees, it's a red flag. Any company genuinely interested in hiring you should welcome an extensive evaluation of what they are offering. And that includes allowing you to engage in conversations with your future co-workers—or better yet, take several of them to lunch so you can chat outside the work environment.

Keep in mind there are a few exceptions for being denied the chance to meet and mingle with future co-workers.

1. You'll be replacing a current manager or another employee who is currently on the job, and the existing employee doesn't know they're on the way out.

2. The working environment is a high-security facility, and your presence could compromise the integrity of proprietary information or processes. (Yes, you can agree to sign a non-disclosure agreement, but if you end up going to work for a competitor, how long will what you learned remain a secret?)

If you run into either one of these roadblocks, ask if you can meet with at least two co-workers at a location away from the work-place. If a supervisor must be in attendance, and you get the feeling that he or she is preventing a candid and honest flow of conversation, ask the employees if they would mind an after-work phone call if you have future questions. Promise you won't be a pest or ask for more than five minutes while on the phone. Yes, this is a bit unorthodox, but obtaining uncensored feedback from those who know the day-to-day drill is essential.

Eliminate any company that rules its employees with Draconian oversight. Based on the type of work being done, this can be a very subjective observation. But if your work-place visit makes you uncomfortable because of picky or overly-zealous rules concerning the use of cell phones, personal items in your workspace, email, dress codes, internet use, or the need for a doctor's verification to take a sick day, ask yourself if that's the kind of environment you want to work in. Rules designed to restrict distractions, inhibit physical movement, or promote conformity, are not only an indication of a poorly managed company; they reflect poorly on the people who work there. Are they such an unprofessional, rowdy bunch that restrictive rules are necessary?

Determine if the company is a good match for your income expectations. That goes for both now and in the future. As new engineering college graduates, my senior class constantly compared salaries offered by the largest employers. These included giants like GE, Westinghouse, Texas Instruments, Allied Chemical, and Motorola. In our minds, the starting salary was a default consideration. In other words, if a company was offering less than the minimum average threshold for graduate engineers, we gave them secondary consideration— or outright disqualified them. The starting annual salary was our first and highest priority in our evaluation of prospective employers.

And it was a perfect example of being short-sighted.

The better way to evaluate an offer of compensation? If your income goal after five-years of working is $200K, you should make sure the company under consideration has employees currently making that level of income who have the same capabilities, education, and experience you'll possess five-years in the future. And just as important, you need the

17

assurance there will be room for you when you're ready to ascend to those levels of responsibility and compensation.

For example, if your research reveals the only employees making $200K are two vice-presidents, what events would have to occur to ensure you have access to one of those positions in five-years? Are those events realistic?

Keep your longer-term goals in mind. While a company may not meet your five-year expectations for income, there are still plenty of reasons to take the job—as long as those reasons directly apply to *you*. Maybe you're looking for a stepping stone, a place to gain experience and obtain the credentials you need to move to another, more appropriate employer.

If the job can serve as a spring-board to bring you closer to where you eventually want to be, the annual starting salary is not your *highest* priority. However, if the company represents the very best employer in your chosen field or industry, and it's where you want to spend as much of your career as possible—*and yet, the salary doesn't meet your expectations*—you may need to re-evaluate the priority you've placed on income.

Determine what drives the company's "big picture" reality. Look at its history. Has it purchased smaller entities and converted them into divisions after spinning off products and people deemed non-profitable? Has it made a practice of laying-off highly paid employees and replacing them with less costly new hires? If so, the company worships profit, and you and your future value to the company will be evaluated accordingly.

For example, if you're an independent, balls-to-the-wall, take no prisoners, win at any cost, kind of guy or gal, and you go to work for a company whose highest values reflect conformity to the system, you're going to be miserable. Conversely, if you enjoy structure, meeting procedural standards, and thrive in an atmosphere with a high level of organization, the same company could be the perfect fit.

Privately held versus public ownership . . . Does it make a difference? Never underestimate the importance of *who* owns the company. A privately-held firm will tend to favor family and close friends for coveted management positions—even when a non-family employee has shown themselves to be more capable. In many private—and typically smaller—companies, the most important factor for advancement is a blood-tie. It's not unusual for the majority stockholder in a private company to also be the CEO. In this situation, there is often the common understanding that a favored son or daughter will be the guaranteed successor. So unless you plan on marrying the owner's daughter or son, your advancement in a closely held company may be limited by a lack of kindship.

There is, however, one offsetting advantage offered by a private company that few larger companies can offer. In general, your ability and talents will be noticed sooner and more rapidly rewarded. Even if top management positions are limited to those with a family relationship, there's usually less bureaucratic structure and fewer politics to deal with—to a point. So if a small private enterprise is at the top of your list, the benefits of rapid recognition and advancement might outweigh the limited access to a chief management position. Just keep in mind that while a divisional or regional manager's job at a private company may be available to you in half the time (compared to a Fortune five-hundred), that may be as far as you'll go. If a vice-presidency is what you want, and history indicates these jobs only go to family members, you'll have to look elsewhere.

What is your gut telling you? When you think about working there, are you excited? Or are you wondering if there's a better choice? If, after doing as much research as possible, and hopefully visiting the office or facility in which you'll be working, you still have concerns—about your immediate boss, the potential for advancement, or the working hours or conditions—it's time to take another look at the specifics.

First, determine if your concerns are really about the job, or if some aspect of the work jeopardizes a healthy life-work balance. For example, if weekend work is required and you're not prepared to give up a half-day on Saturday, the company isn't the problem, it's your priorities. If your personal time is more important than your career, then any job that involves weekend work is going to generate the same concerns. If that's the case, you'll need to redefine which industries and type of work are a better "fit" for your personal priorities.

Just as important, if you've got "red flags" going up over the specific nature of the job or you feel uncomfortable with the expectations of management because their criteria for evaluation is too subjective, vague, or conflicts with your values and beliefs, you need to face the truth: The job isn't right for you.

Don't confuse immediate ego-gratification with long term opportunity. It's one of the biggest mistakes you can make: Taking a job because it represents a prominent position with a prestigious firm, and yet, you know you'll have to force yourself to tolerate the day-to-date work because it's not what you really want to do.

Don't let your ego make you miserable. If there's even the slightest chance your choice of employer is driven by the need to impress or influence others, or to gain the respect and recognition of your friends or family, read the next paragraph very carefully.

Those who truly care about you will want you to choose a job that makes you happy. *Others could give a rat's ass about your success.* Remember, the more success you achieve, the more your fair-weather friends will distance themselves from you. They will not want to be reminded of their own frustrating, mediocre existence. Make sure you really want the experience of what you're going after and not just the IDEA of having it because of how you will impress or influence others around you.

Still struggling with the decision? Unsure where the problem lies? Ask yourself the following:

1. **Why are you considering this particular job?** Make sure you're intentions are driven by a love of the work, participating in the daily grind, and feeling good about yourself and how you'll be spending your time.

2. **Are you ready to commit to the work?** Good intentions won't pay the bills. You may fully *intend* to give it everything you've got, but all those good intentions won't matter one iota if you don't have the motivation, stamina, and actions to get the work done.

3. **Is this something you could do for the next two, five, ten, or even twenty years?** No, it's not meant to sound like a jail sentence, but spending that length of time working at the same company shouldn't feel like one, either. Yes, you can always quit later if things "don't work out," but that approach usually means you haven't done enough research or you're not ready to fully commit.

I'll finish this chapter with a note about change in general: Make sure you're not misinterpreting the general anxiety you feel about a life-changing event—a new job or career shift—as a warning about a specific company or the circumstances of the workplace. It's normal to experience some apprehension over starting a new job, especially if it involves moving to a different location. That kind of anxiety comes from anticipating the unknown effects of change, and in this case, it's the normal resistance we feel when thinking about that uncomfortable period of adjustment while we learn where the bathroom is located, find the best place to eat lunch, and deal with the idiosyncrasies of new co-workers.

Do your best to separate your general feelings about relocating, leaving friends and family, and acclimating to a new routine or location, from the actual work and the company environment.

If you're still unsure about your decision, but can't turn the job down without wondering if you're making a mistake, the only way you may ever know if the position is right for you is to accept it—conditionally. This means making an agreement with *yourself* to accept the offer and work for two or three months, then re-evaluate, using the same questions and vetting methods above. You may need as much as six months to make an accurate evaluation, but take the time and learn what you didn't know before accepting the job.

For some, this approach may represent an ethical dilemma, but I assure you, the company is hiring you on the same basis. There are no guarantees, and any offer of employment is conditional on performance and adaptability. There's no reason not to make that arrangement a two-way street. Just make sure to keep your side of the on-going evaluation confidential.

(Note: This suggestion comes with its own sets of risks, specifically of being labeled a "job hopper." I'll go into detail about what this means and how it can affect your career in a later chapter.)

Chapter Three
What's Your Employee "Type?"

What Type of Employee Are You . . . Loyalist or User?

I've known plenty of folks who described their relationship with their employer as "still developing," or "we're both waiting to see how it works out."

Many had no formal career plan, or if they did, it was something along the lines of, "Do my job, keep my head down, and finish out my thirty years with a huge 401K." Throughout their career, their job responsibilities seldom changed, and after being snubbed several times for promotion, they'd settled in for the long haul, never thinking their future was always at risk from buy-outs, re-organization, or company-wide layoffs.

Today's smart corporate employee knows their relationship with the company is ultimately temporary. Sure, we talk about long-term commitment, longevity, and the value of loyalty. However, to have any real meaning, those ideas have to work in both directions. Realistic employees have learned to evaluate a company's promise of tomorrow with a lot of skepticism.

Today is what counts. Tomorrow is what you must prepare for.

To have a productive relationship with your employer—both from the standpoint of the company meeting your expectations and you being able to move your career in the direction you want it to go—I recommend determining which category, or "type" of employee that best fits your mindset and future goals. Then you can evaluate new work opportunities originating from both inside and outside your current employer to determine the best fit for your personal circumstances and situation.

For our purposes, let's define the work relationship into two categories: The "Loyalist," and the "User."

A *Loyalist* is committed to developing and accomplishing their career goals with their current employer. They are completely "on-board" with the company's programs, policies, and direction. They have no plans to seek alternative employment from another source and can see themselves retiring from the company in thirty years as a top-level executive.

The Loyalist guy or gal brings the same level of commitment to their work (and their employer) as if they owned the company. When it comes to company business and activities, they're "all in," dedicating the majority of their time and attention to their employer's advantage. I've heard some Loyalists describe it as being able to do exactly what they've always wanted to do and having found the perfect vehicle by which to do it.

Here are the typical characteristics of a Loyalist:

1. They use their investment money to buy stock in the company because financial ownership makes it real.

2. They have identified and targeted the next job or promotion level for their career path and are actively developing the skills and acquiring the experience to achieve it. They regularly ask their supervisor for the opportunity to assume new responsibilities, knowing it's the key to moving up within the organization.

3. They help others to complete their tasks and assignments. I'm not talking about doing the actual work but offering suggestions and direction when help is needed. They assist co-workers and subordinates without expecting to receive immediate acknowledgment or credit. They know it's only a

matter of time before the positive effect of their efforts will be noticed by management.

4. They're familiar with the concept of team building and the process of directing and utilizing the talents and abilities of multiple individuals rather than focusing on one superstar.

5. They know the profit margins and market share of the products and services sold by their company. In short, they recognize the source of the money. They also have a handle on the cost of manufacture, sales, delivery, returns, warranty replacement, and spoilage, if the product has a limited shelf life. They can talk intelligently about new and potential markets using the parameters of demographics, competition, emerging technology, and other metrics specific to their industry. If they have sales or marketing responsibility, they can cite their customer's annual sales, market share, possible future competitive threats, and can suggest at least three ways to increase their business. (If you think this kind of information is impossible to get, you're not ready for the corner office.)

6. They are familiar with promotional and advertising budgets, the return on those expenditures, and how their company's budget compares to the competition.

7. They know "who's who" in the company. They're familiar with the names and responsibilities of middle and upper management, how long they've been employed at their current position, their previous employers, career path, job assignments, and educational background. They also know their birthdays and anniversary dates.

8. They offer praise and feedback to co-workers and subordinates, both privately and in front of supervision and management. They NEVER criticize another co-worker in front of others. And when the boss privately asks them what they think of another employee, they use tact and diplomacy, indicating the future can always hold improvement.

9. They attend all company events and functions, whether business-related or social. They realize their absence from any company event will be conspicuous—not something they want management to notice. They know that corporate social functions are often used as a testing ground, to see who rises to the top, handles themselves well, and demonstrates leadership ability.

10. They ask for more training, then volunteer to teach the same class or seminar to other employees. If appropriate, they offer to present the material to customers, modifying the content or curriculum to make it more suitable or applicable for the specific audience. In effect, "training" becomes their middle name. They may decide to publish a monthly newsletter with industry updates or send out a weekly or even a daily email with tips and ideas for increasing sales, or reducing wasteful, time-consuming activities.

Sound overwhelming? It isn't. Not when it's planned, managed, and scheduled. Remember, you have your entire career to work on it—because you're *all in*.

What about "Users?" How do they fit into the framework of the corporation? A *User* has no interest in a long-term relationship with their current employer and is exploiting the company as a springboard to other opportunities. They see their employer as a place to acquire knowledge about the industry and marketplace—then move on, either to another company or to start their own business.

They may also be in a holding pattern, unwilling to commit to their current position because they're actively looking for other opportunities. Having accepted their current job for financial reasons, or because they believed they would be more employable if they were already employed (usually true), they're waiting for a better job.

If you fall into the User category, here are a few suggestions to receive the greatest return from the time you spend with your current employer:

1. **Know exactly what is expected of you.** Understand your job responsibilities and how your performance is measured, then include any subjective considerations your manager is likely to impose, based on how you perceive her values. Your goal is to gain the reputation of a reliable employee who does acceptable work *for the position for which you were hired.* Having said that, never use your job description as an excuse for failing to meet your manager's escalating expectations. Job descriptions are notoriously vague and seldom encompass the full range of responsibilities and activities that comprise a job well-done.

2. **Determine the most advanced job title or position you would be comfortable performing, then be ready to move up**. Do your best to convey an attitude of wanting a promotion and the greater responsibility that comes with it. This will go a long way in being seen as a valuable company asset and receiving positive evaluations and raises.

3. **Make no enemies and cultivate as many positive business relationships as you can.** Always be aware of new networking opportunities. Grow and strengthen your network with regular communication. Let them know you're available to help or provide professional assistance, even if it's outside the definition of your job description. Many of these contacts will be customers. Some you may never meet in person, due to distance, restricted outside mobility, or the need to adhere to appropriate professional protocol. Just be sure to treat all of them with equal value, because you don't know when the billing clerk on the other end of the phone will turn out to be an important influencer's son or daughter.

(True story: The new guy supervising the loading dock was being bossy as hell, and since it was his first day on the job, I was tempted to suggest he take his belligerent attitude down a notch, especially when he demanded I move my car because he didn't want "vendors" parking on that side of the building. I decided to let it go. I moved my car and went inside, where I learned that the "new guy" had just married the owner's daughter and was learning the business from the ground up.)

4. **Don't overlook the influence your co-workers can have on your future success.** Always be patient, courteous, and friendly. Talking down to a co-worker or being belligerent can earn you the reputation of an asshole—or worse, an arrogant asshole. Instead, learn the birthdays of your fellow employees and send them a card. Congratulate them on promotions and advancements. Your co-workers know and can influence many people in and outside the company, and one of them could be a vital link to a better position if and when you decide to leave.

5. **Be a team player.** This is a logical extension of number three. Never miss an opportunity to share credit for your success. Even if it's nothing more than acknowledging the administrative staff for their help in putting together your presentation, always include anyone and everyone that was involved in the process. Management will love you for it. We all have the desire to be singularly identified for our accomplishments and to receive the accolades that go along with it, but corporate super-stars are quick to burn out, while *team players* tend to stay in the game much longer. This isn't counter-intuitive to the ultimate goal of moving on to a different employer or starting your own business; it ensures that the decision to leave is made by *you*, and only when you're ready to leave.

6. **Volunteer to help your boss.** Let your supervisor know you're always available to pitch in and help with the workload,

especially when she's overloaded with planning, year-end reports, trade shows, promotional events, and other time-intensive activities. Building this kind of rapport with your supervisor will help motivate her to write glowing reviews of your work, recommend you for raises and promotions, and increase the likelihood of cutting you some slack in the event your production lags for a short period.

7. At work, be present and focused on your job. If you're obviously distracted, or others see you seemingly always busy with personal phone calls, social media, or email, you're taking a huge risk. From the company's viewpoint, you're not only wasting their time and money; you're abusing it. Conversely, demonstrating concern over deadlines, customer problems and complaints, and taking responsibility to help out in a crisis, will get you remembered and rewarded.

8. Be on time. Never be the one who forces others—especially your boss—to wait. Being late for meetings and appointments is the quickest way to lose respect and acquire the reputation of someone who doesn't put enough priority on company business. There's no excuse for being late. If your internal time clock doesn't cooperate, schedule your arrival time for fifteen minutes early. If that's not enough, keep adding fifteen-minute buffers until you're consistently the first one to show up. Remember, there's no middle ground when it comes to punctuality. Making others wait is disrespectful and rude. Conversely, it makes a great impression on management to find a subordinate ready and prepared to start when they arrive.

9. Be positive – always! You're the guy or gal who's great to be around, and others appreciate your positive spin. During my stint as co-owner of a large photography company, part of my job was to call on school principals to present our products and services. Time and time again, I saw a sign with the same message placed over the doorway of the school's administration offices: "Attitude is Everything." It's a simple concept, but it's hard to overestimate its power.

10. **Keep your plans to yourself.** Not in it for the long haul? *Never* share your intentions to leave the company, even if your departure date is years in the future. Management must believe you're indefinitely committed to your job. If they discover your true intentions are not aligned with theirs, they will put you on the shortlist for termination through lay-offs, downsizing, or "managing out."

Now, let's compare the recommended suggestions for Loyalists versus Users. Notice the differences between the two lists? (Hint: It's a trick question.) Based on the standpoint of your everyday activities and behavior, I'm sure you've realized there's more similarity than disparity. And that's the point. You could combine the lists without any real conflict.

Here's why that's important: Based on your behavior, and as far as management and co-workers can tell, *there should be no outward or obvious clues that could reveal your personal agenda.*

Regardless of whether you fall under the category of User or Loyalist (or somewhere in-between), your relationship with an employer should fit within a much larger picture—a personally-crafted life-plan—driven by your financial objectives, your need for autonomy and independence, and a preferred level of balance between your work and personal life.

This is a drastic difference from the traditional employee mindset in which workers have historically depended upon the company to determine his or her fate. An employee who chooses a *My Life First* mindset does their best to influence their career path within the company, but they know it is ultimately up to them to determine their professional destiny.

Now for the big question . . .

Which type of employee are you? And more important, which approach makes more sense for your future? Knowing this upfront will make it much easier to make the decisions that inevitably confront every employee: Do I take the promotion? Should I move to the new location? Do I stay with my current employer, or should I accept the job offer from a competitor?

If you're not sure which category is the best choice for your circumstances, don't worry. We're just getting started. Before we're finished, you'll have a much better idea of your expectations and whether the company you're with can reasonably satisfy them.

Chapter Four
Yes, Money Matters!

Your total compensation, including your annual salary, benefits, and perks, is a reflection of your relative value to your employer. I say *relative* because the method of determining an employee's annual compensation is usually based on factors that extend beyond the individual's actual productivity–in dollars and cents–at any specific point in time. (Yes, there are exceptions, but these are typically commission-based salespeople, whose pay is directly related mathematically to their sales volume.)

We'll talk about each of these factors, but first, let's discuss how your *employer's* expectations impact your salary.

If you're just starting your working career, your employer's expectations are substantially different than for someone with several years of experience in the same industry. As a new employee with little or no familiarity with the job, your first year is about two things: (1) Learning the ropes, and (2) Proving yourself to management by substantiating their decision to hire you.

As a new hire, you'll be expected to learn the skills, processes, and procedures associated with your job function, and become intimately familiar with the company and your place within it. Proving yourself to management will be a cumulative process of convincing your supervisor of your dedication and long term intentions to serve the company's interests.

During the first few months, you may not have the opportunity to show off your talent directly in the form of customer interactions or with direct, hands-on accountability. However, your boss will always be looking for growth in areas of professional competence. She'll want to see you making consistent progress toward assuming your full job responsibilities and accomplishing the routine duties of your assignment with as little supervision as possible.

Some companies call this a probationary period, the new-hire period, or the initial employment period. During this initial or "trial" phase, your compensation is often little more than a payment toward your future value. As far as the company is concerned, your work doesn't justify your salary because you're not working at peak productivity. You're receiving training, orientation, and gaining experience—at the company's expense—that will eventually give you the tools and knowledge you need to perform the function for which you were hired. The fact that they're paying you during this period means they're investing in the employee you'll become.

If you're in sales, you may also find your participation in bonus and commission programs on a temporary hold until you've completed training. I've also seen sales incentive programs that payout on a staggered or increasing percentage over time (usually a year to eighteen months) until you're being paid one hundred percent of your production bonus.

Asking for a raise during a probation period is career suicide. Unless there are mitigating circumstances comparable to your rich uncle buying out the company, you'll need to wait until you can show what you're made of.

Think you're the exception? It's a common delusion. Here's a short example:

Acme sales engineer "Bob," was determined to push the salary envelope from the day he was hired. Because of an unusual circumstance (an unplanned vacancy), he was offered an opportunity to take over a remote branch office right after completing the company's formal training course. With only four months on the job, this was a real opportunity—and a challenge.

After accepting the new position, he immediately scheduled a meeting with his manager. He planned to demand a raise that was—in his opinion—commensurate with his new responsibility. As he left for the meeting, he turned to me and said, "And the boss had better not insult my ass with a ten percent raise."

He had nothing to worry about. His ass was never insulted with a raise of any kind; instead, it was given a good verbal kick to ensure he recognized the difference between an opportunity to prove himself and the payment of tribute to placate his ego.

Yes, he admitted that money was discussed, but just long enough to dismiss the idea. The boss responded with, "We'll talk about it on your anniversary date. That's eight months from now. That'll give you plenty of time to get organized, meet the customers, and begin to produce some business."

In short, he was saying, "Prove yourself first, then we'll talk money."

Without a record of performance and productivity, there was nothing to substantiate Bob's request for a raise based on merit. Even eight months later, the increase Bob received was little more than a cost of living adjustment, because it was simply too soon for the company to make a long-term financial commitment in exchange for future-based productivity.

Fact: Increases in compensation result from establishing your long-term value. In most industries, paying for a specific accomplishment is not the way the system works (unless, as I mentioned before, your compensation is based wholly on commission). While you may receive a boost in your annual bonus for an outstanding accomplishment or meeting a productivity goal, your permanent salary increases are paced to reflect your long term value to the company.

Here's the company's reasoning: Just because you rocked it this year and increased the company's business or profitability, doesn't mean you're going to do it next year. And the company knows it. So they look at a long term average of what you're worth to the company's bottom line, and they make that evaluation knowing they could replace you—*typically for less money*—if they needed to.

This usually means raises in salary are contingent upon longevity factored by your ability to demonstrate consistent, long-term performance. Does that mean it's always necessary to put in the time before expecting a large salary bump? Like I said, that's the usual situation. However, there's an alternative to outright asking for a raise that can help accelerate a hike in your income.

Instead of a raise, ask for more responsibility. This strategy communicates your desire to be more involved in company operations and growth. It also diminishes the negative impact of asking for more without proving yourself deserving. You're not asking for more money to maintain your status quo workload. You're saying you're ready to assume more responsibility—your silent request for additional compensation is understood.

Now, here's what makes this strategy interesting. Declaring your desire to become a more valuable asset to the company usually makes you more valuable—immediately. *In fact, your perceived attitude is often more important to your compensation and longevity than your future actions, whether you deliver or not.*

Asking for more responsibility can be a defining moment in your career and should not be left to chance. It's most effective when revealed as a personal or professional goal during a formal performance review. If you have several years of outstanding productivity under your belt, you may even want to suggest a possible target date for promotion—typically a year in the future—then ask your boss if this is realistic. If your manager tells you promotions are limited or currently unavailable, your response should be something along the lines of, "I'd still like to work toward the goal. Even though an opening may not be available for some time, when it does, I'll be ready."

If you're willing to make a geographic move, say so. While you may want to mention any regional preferences you might have, avoid reciting a list of places where you don't want to live. It's an indication your request for a promotion is conditional, and in effect, you're already turning down any future offers the company might make that requires a move to a personally undesirable area.

It's a good idea to periodically determine what you're worth. Most industries have an average amount of compensation for a specific job function. One way to determine yours is by joining professional organizations related to your Industry. Membership benefits may provide access to organizational data that often includes the current range of salary and compensation, based on job type.

If you perform a sales function, the process is even easier. First, determine your compensation as a percentage of the total amount of sales you generate annually. Be sure to include the replacement value (a dollar amount) for health and life insurance, company contributions to a retirement fund, 401K, or other investment plans, personal use of a company vehicle if provided, and any reward-related travel and trips.

Finally, add in the value or replacement cost of any personal advantages you receive from using company assets, including reimbursable expenses from which you derive some personal benefit. It's easy to overlook these "minor conveniences," but that's because we take them for granted, forgetting the actual cost of calculators, phones, writing pads, desk pens, business cards, and even that morning cup of coffee waiting in the break room. All of these "perks" are something that self-employed entrepreneurs must pay for.

Now compare this total to the national average for compensating an independent sales force in the same industry. For example, if 6% of gross sales is the national average paid to independent sales reps for selling blue widgets, and you're currently receiving three and a half percent as compensation for selling your company's version of a blue widget, you can bet your company knows it. And while you can ask for an increase to close some of the gap, it's doubtful you'll ever receive one hundred percent of the difference. And that's intentional.

Why?

First, that six percent commission is gross compensation. It's the total amount a rep receives. And from that, the expenses of an office, administrative services, transportation and travel, computers, phones, office supplies, and all the other requirements of running a business are paid. What's leftover is the rep's compensation.

There's a second reason, and while it's not as obvious, it's just as important . . . *you and the company MUST have headroom for future salary growth.*

Topping out at a "salary ceiling" removes the incentive to do more. If you know you've received all the compensation available to you—regardless of how much more business you produce—how motivated will you be to exceed last year's productivity by twenty percent?

Yes, many companies have bonus programs designed to pay for year-over-year increases, and on the off-chance your employer has an equitable bonus program to reward those who increase company sales and profit, count yourself lucky. But in most cases, as an employee, your total annual compensation—including bonuses—will usually lag behind the gross commission paid to an independent sales rep doing the same level of business.

How do the majority of companies rationalize this "income-gap?" To offset the shortfall, management wants you to believe there are other "value-added" employee benefits that more than compensates for the difference. Most of these tend to fall under the category of the subjective and conceptual, including job security(?), company identity and status, educational resources and support, and the illusion that the company is there for you, and even in a difficult economy, they've got your back.

Do any of these things have any actual value? In a word, *No*. At least not the kind of value you can put a number on. And keep this caveat in mind: What many employees mistakenly identify as intangible benefits are more accurately described as a hesitancy to relinquish the familiarity with the status quo combined with a fear of the unknown. Said another way, it's a concern that a new job may not provide the same level of comfort or satisfaction provided by the current work environment.

Before we can dive a bit deeper into the comparison between a corporate employee's compensation and an entrepreneur doing the same type of work, it's important to understand how large corporations view and administer employee compensation.

A large company operates on a forecasted budget, with its workforce salary being one of its most significant expenses. The company has the on-going obligation to meet an employee's expectations of receiving a monthly paycheck on time, every time. But does that obligation also extend to sharing the company's profits? No, that's reserved for the stockholders or private owners.

"But that's not fair," you say. In your opinion, those profits were the direct result of your efforts, and as far as you're concerned, you should share in the spoils of victory.

Rather than argue the point, let's look at the situation when your productivity *falls.* For this example, let's say your salary is 100K a year. You earn it by being a good mid-level manager. You meet management's expectations and can demonstrate a record of sustained and study growth in market share and customer retention. This year, you and your team brought in several new large accounts, adding thirty percent to your total business volume as compared to last year.

"I should be paid more money for that," you say. "My efforts were directly responsible for putting more profit in the company coffers, and it's only fair that I share in the financial gain."

It's a strong argument, based on logic and the bottom line. But before you march into your supervisor's office and demand "what's rightfully yours," keep reading.

Let's jump a year into the future. Those new accounts you and your team brought in have decided to revert to their previous supplier. Maybe their decision was based on your company's inability to meet the requested price or delivery, or one of your salespeople pissed off someone in the purchasing group. Regardless of the reason, you've lost those new accounts. But that's not all. Your most productive salesperson got an offer from your number one competitor and decided to leave, and her customers chose to follow her.

Now you're numbers suck. You're down forty percent compared to last year, and even if you factor out the loss of the new accounts, you're still down a good ten percent due to your previously loyal customers switching brands to maintain their relationship with your ex-employee.

Should you expect an immediate salary cut to sixty thousand a year?

Seldom do large companies penalize their employees with reductions in annual base compensation. If the loss of business was preventable or resulted from incompetence or irresponsible behavior, they might (and probably would) terminate and replace. However, if the lost business was truly beyond your control, it's doubtful they would take that kind of drastic action.

It's very likely they would continue to send the same paycheck, in the same amount, every month. And so you—a mid-level manager with sucky numbers—would continue to pay your bills while maintaining the same lifestyle and income expectations you've always had.

Large companies pay their people based on the long haul. Employers know there's going to be good years and bad, with a few outstanding years thrown in to help boost the average. And that's also how they calculate employee compensation. The good years provide a cushion of cash for the not-so-good years. Peak and valleys are always averaged to show a more accurate representation of the marketplace. Instead of the periodic ups and downs, it's the trend that's important. Steady growth over time. Just like the way a corporate salary is administered.

Although this is a relatively straightforward concept, you can't believe the number of employees who lose sight of the big picture. Even those who receive a portion of their compensation in the form of a bonus or commission often feel slighted when comparing the dollars they received to the gross dollar value of the business they generated. In effect, it's like an investor who becomes obsessed with the day-to-day performance of his portfolio rather than the long term growth.

"But my base salary hasn't moved up in several years," you argue. "They're taking me for granted."

Yes, there are always exceptions, so let's do the math. If your job assignment provides you with a direct correlation between your performance and salary (again, sales is always an excellent example), and you can rationalize an annual income of $150,000—based on your long-term, historical performance—but you only receive $120,000, that's thirty grand a year you're stockpiling for the company's benefit.

But that doesn't necessarily mean you're being underpaid. To know for sure, you'll need to compare your compensation to your competitive counterpart, both inside and outside your company (within the same industry).

If all mid-level managers are making about the same as you, regardless of performance, then the answer is simple: Your company is using a functional compensation system. In short, you're being paid to perform a function, and that's the value your company is willing to pay to get it done. While there's little doubt your productivity in dollars and cents is worth more, your company hasn't structured their compensation program to recognize a direct relationship between productivity and compensation, at least not for your specific position.

Does that mean it's time to start sending out your resume?

Not necessarily. And certainly not immediately. The first year you recognize a discrepancy between your compensation and productivity, use your performance to justify asking for a raise at your next review. You're not going to ask for the entire shortfall, but half of it is a reasonable request. And no, that doesn't mean you should expect to receive half. It's just a place to start the negotiations.

If the company wants to keep you, they may grant you an increase. Then again, they may not, especially if meeting your request raises your income above the "norm" for your industry position or job description.

If you like your job and want to stay, accept the situation for now and track your performance for another year. Remember, the company evaluates your performance in the long term, which is also the way they pay you. You may need more time (history) to rationalize your request as being commensurate with the longer-term averaging of the peaks and valleys of your performance.

But what if, after three or more years, you find yourself continuing to fall behind in compensation? It happens. The productivity of true superstars can easily outstrip the company's capacity to pay for consistently outstanding work. If you find yourself in this situation—your performance significantly and repeatedly exceeds other company employees in the same position, and yet, you're paid an amount similar to that received by your co-workers—it's an indication you've outgrown your job.

Bottom line, your company does not have a payment structure to compensate you and other exceptional employees like you.

Your first clue will be management's attempt to justify their refusal for a salary increase by citing the limitations of the pay range associated with your position. And if a promotion isn't available due to a lack of room at the next level, your manager may try to placate you with promises of long-term career positioning and the virtues of patience.

The result? You begin to feel the effects of negative motivation, resulting from management's determined stand to ignore the obvious incongruences in your compensation by feigning indifference and disinterest when confronted with the numbers.

How long do you allow your compensation to lag behind your performance before you take action? Knowing when to draw the line is different for each individual. It depends on your personal situation, professional goals, and job alternatives.

As I mentioned above, allowing a substantial lag in compensation to go on too long will eventually affect your attitude and performance. While you may tell yourself you're building future job security, it's a hard pill to swallow, especially when you realize your future employment is always subject to the silent risk of termination from buy-outs, reorganization, and lay-offs.

In general, after three years of taking it in the shorts, it's time to evaluate your relationship with your employer. You can start by finding out what you're worth on the open market. Being able to show a history of consistent growth in sales, profit, and productivity is a valuable commodity, and if your current employer refuses to pay you for it, a competitor usually will.

What about using third-party leverage to boost your income? Right up front, I want to say that I don't recommend this. Yes, I'll admit this method has the potential to immediately raise your income after other methods have failed. However, the process is risky, and if your real intentions are discovered, you can damage your reputation and even lose your job.

That being said, I know there are plenty of readers who are going to try it, so I'll give you an overview of the process and point out as many caution flags as I can.

Here's how it works:

The goal is to generate an offer from a competitor and use it as leverage to get your current employer to match it. You shouldn't consider this tactic unless you've been with the company at least three years, have an outstanding track record, and your compensation is significantly behind the norm for your industry. In other words, the company has refused to compensate you commensurately for your productivity and needs to be "shocked" into the reality of what you're really worth.

Here's your first red flag, and this is vital: *Never reveal that you went "shopping" to produce an offer.* Your manager must believe the competitor approached you—not the other way around—and the offer came to you out of the blue. Ideally, you're trying to create a bidding war to drive your compensation as high as possible. However, in reality, that rarely happens. About the best you can hope for is that your company will match the competition's (higher) offer. This assumes your current employer wants to keep you and recognizes your value as a long-term asset.

How do you generate an offer from a competitor? By letting the competition know *indirectly* that you would entertain the idea of leaving your current job. One way to start the ball rolling is to casually mention it to neutral third parties—customers, distributors, end-users, and OEMS who are always in contact with the competition. An off-hand comment to their purchasing group, salespeople, or internal management is an excellent way of passing along your interest. Just make sure to convey your interest in a subtle if not subliminal way.

Here's an example of how to drop the hint: "I've noticed the folks over at XYZ Corporation seem to be happy with the compensation program and like the direction the company is headed. I've also heard the local branch has a great manager. It's always good to hear about a company that treats its people right."

Your goal is to solicit a question or comment similar to this: "I happen to know the manager at XYZ, and if you'd like, I'd be glad to mention you to him."

Your response? "I'm always interested in talking to great companies. Of course, I'd appreciate it if this remains confidential, just between you and me."

If you want to push the envelope and be a little more aggressive, convey your interest to someone you trust and who has a personal or business relationship with a competitor. Simply ask them to communicate your interest while stressing the absolute necessity for confidentiality. And remember, you're never looking for a job, *you're in the process of re-evaluating your career.* The key is to always have plausible deniability in the event your current employer discovers you've been talking to the competition.

If you're well-known and well-liked in your local market, it's not unusual to receive a phone call from a competitor inviting you to lunch or to have a drink after work. Thank the caller for the interest, accept the invitation, and say nothing else on the phone.

During the meeting, keep your comments light and social. You don't need to sell yourself. The competition already knows about your skill and ability. Otherwise, they wouldn't be talking to you. Ask a few questions: What are their most critical needs in the local market? Are there any future plans for reorganization? Will upcoming promotions or vacancies create changes in the local office management? Preface your questions by saying you understand if they can't provide specific answers without a working commitment, but they're subjects to talk more about as both parties move closer to a decision. Also mention that your relationship with your current employer has been positive; however, you believe it's a good time to take a look at the current opportunities in the industry.

If the competition has a place for you (or can create one), it's not unusual to see an offer within a week or two. Express your appreciation as soon as you receive it, then ask for several days to think it over.

Next, schedule a meeting with your manager as soon as possible. If your boss questions you about how the offer was originated, or how much contact you've had with the competition, downplay your answer by saying, "I ran into the XYZ regional manager at one of our distributors a couple of weeks ago. He was cordial, and we exchanged a few comments about the weather. I understand he asked the purchasing agent a few questions about me. I think they have a vacancy they need to fill, and the urgency of the situation prompted them to approach me."

If you have an inside staff job, say that a business acquaintance recommended you for a vacancy and the competition's interest has taken you entirely by surprise.

Now it's time to talk to your manager about money—*indirectly*. The emphasis should be on how much you enjoy your present job, the working environment, and especially the relationship you have with your boss—she's your mentor, champion, and friend. Add that you had always imagined your career advancement taking place within your current company, and this new offer has resulted in some sleepless nights.

Then it's your boss's turn to talk. Don't interrupt. Don't contradict. And don't ask for her opinion (what would she do?). If she wants to keep you, she'll express how valuable you've been to the company. She'll also express how much she wants you to stay. And initially, she'll probably do it without offering to meet the competition's offer. It's her job to retain talented, productive employees and do it as inexpensively as possible.

By the end of the conversation, if your boss fails to offer a monetary consideration to entice you to remain with the company, mention how the additional money isn't everything, and yet, it's a consideration you can't ignore. Your sights are on the long term, and that includes a rewarding financial relationship with your employer. If there's room for negotiation, you'd like to discuss it.

Then shut-up and listen. What your supervisor says next will offer clues about your perceived value to the company and what future plans, if any, they have for you.

Now, let's look at the other side of the situation. What if the competitor's offer is so good you're tempted to consider it?

Keep in mind there are other benefits to be gained—other than a salary bump—by staying with your current employer. By turning down an offer from a competitor, *without* an increase in compensation, you're displaying your loyalty and commitment. Corporations love that kind of dedication, and yes, a few are willing to pay for it—in the long term.

Others, however, are not.

Either they won't be pressured into a game of "match the offer or lose me," or the current corporate policy makes it impossible to pay more for the job function, regardless of the employee's productivity.

That's why you can't always expect a counteroffer to stay. Keep this in mind if you're tempted to "play hardball" in negotiating a salary increase. You might inadvertently negotiate yourself out of a job you really wanted to keep.

Finally, make your decision on how it will affect the next five years of your life—financially, emotionally, and yes, even physically. Don't forget to evaluate the opportunities for advancement a new employer can offer that can't be matched by your current company. Keep in mind that if you make the decision to leave, and you inform your boss of your intentions, you're done. Be prepared to walk out that day. Once you make it clear you're moving on, you'll be considered an unwelcome competitive influence that must be removed from the working environment as quickly as possible.

Now let's consider the rare situation of being *overpaid*! Up until now, we've talked about a chronic shortfall in compensation as compared to others employed in the same industry and performing the same function. But what if it's the other way around? What if the math indicates you're being overpaid?

First, be thankful for your unusual good fortune. But before taking the weekend to celebrate, you need to determine the reason. If a higher salary resulted from accepting a move to a different location, or as compensation for taking on more responsibility without a commensurate promotion or title change, that's fine. But if you're getting an extra twenty grand a year because of some vaguely construed relationship—the boss has more than a professional interest in you, you married the vice-president's daughter, or you were hired for a job paying a higher level of compensation, then transferred or reassigned to a position of lesser perceived value—there's a good chance the discrepancy is going to be questioned by those whose job is to bird-dog those kinds of inconsistencies.

Do companies ever adjust your compensation downward to correct the "irregularity?" It's extremely rare. HR knows a financial demotion is demoralizing, and most employees never recover from it. Regardless of the reason for downsizing an employee's income, it becomes a point of endless contention, and the employee seldom lives up to their professional potential afterward. The usual resolution is termination, either by managing out, layoff, or offering the employee a mandatory transfer to a location they know will be unacceptable.

Unfortunately, there's seldom a reasonable compromise or alternative in these kinds of situations, and if you find yourself on the receiving end of an unrealistically high amount of compensation for your job function or position—and there's not reasonable, long-term justification for it—you should consider your longevity with your current employer at risk.

Think I'm a bit of an alarmist?

Corporate truth: You will NOT be allowed to receive compensation that is significantly more than the defined maximum for your job position. (At least, not for very long.)

Quick story: Around my eighth year with Acme, my co-worker, Mr. Split, another sales engineer, decided to leave the company to start his own business. During his last two months with Acme, he spent most of his time negotiating with Arthur Electric, a prime potential customer for Acme's electrical panels and circuit breakers (the metal box on the side of your house where electricity is received from the power company).

At the time, Arthur was one of the largest electrical contractors in the country, which translated into a lot of panels and circuit breakers. Especially circuit breakers—at least a million units a year. With this kind of volume, Arthur expected the absolute lowest price. And after weeks of negotiating, it appeared our company would not be able to meet Arthur's "magic" number.

Essentially giving up on the deal, Mr. Split turned his attention to preparing for his transition from Acme. As the only remaining sales engineer in the office, I inherited the Arthur account as a matter of course. However, I didn't give it much thought since Acme had made it clear they were unable to meet Arthur's bottom line price.

While Mr. Split and I had dismissed the possibility of booking Arthur's business, the wholesale distributor salesman— "Danny," an extremely likable guy who could sell sawdust to a lumberyard—wasn't ready to quit. His company, we'll call it ABC Distributors, would stock the merchandise, deliver

Arthur's orders, and process the billing paperwork. In exchange, ABC would receive a profit in the form of a mark-up. (At the time, most if not all orders from contractors were handled by distributors, who purchased from Acme and re-sold to the final customer.)

Danny was already making regular sales calls on Arthur, selling them conduit, wire, receptacles, and other electrical components. The opportunity to sell panels and breakers to Arthur represented a large potential boost in income, not only for the distributor but for Danny personally. For example, for every nickel the distributor added to the price of a circuit breaker, they would generate at least fifty thousand dollars in annual income, (based on selling a million units).

About a week after Acme had made it clear they were unable to meet Arthur's prices, I received a phone call from Danny. He asked me if I would make one final presentation to Arthur. He specifically wanted me to pitch the quality of our product and the distributor's commitment to provide a back-up stock to prevent shortages of material. He wanted to stress the value of those two benefits when calculated in reduced warranty calls and elimination of work delays from back-ordered components.

After a few phone calls, the purchasing agent agreed to meet with us. I advised Mr. Split of the new meeting, and he told me to "give it my best shot," adding, "but you're probably wasting your time."

After an hour-long presentation, Arthur's purchasing agent was impressed. The idea of saving money by reducing warranty service calls and the elimination of back-orders was appealing to him. Not only from the financial aspect but from the hours it would save in paperwork and administrative follow-up. Rather than being forced to process a predictable number of additional job orders due to component failures with brand X, he could expect a much lower number of warranty call-backs, customer service problems, and reorders by switching to Acme.

He gave us his bottom line number. It was a few pennies higher than the previous price target, but still very low. The distributor salesman was disappointed. He knew the price-point was probably unattainable. But I was familiar enough with our company's production costs to realize there was an opportunity for Acme to benefit from economy of scale. Adding another million circuit breakers to the company's existing production had the potential to raise the profit margin across the board—for all circuit breaker orders.

I presented the numbers to Acme's product manager; emphasizing Arthur's use of Acme breakers would make them a default endorser of Acme products. I topped it off with a pitch to his ego, adding that having the nation's largest residential electrical contractor as a customer would entitle upper management to a lot of bragging rights at future industry conventions.

It took two more weeks of meetings, phone conversations, and number crunching at the corporate level. In the end, the company decided to meet the price and take the business.

Now, here's where the story gets dicey. As a sales engineer, I was paid on a salary plus bonus plan. The amount of my bonus was calculated as a measure of dollars sold against an annual quota. For example, selling a million dollars annually against an assigned quota of the same amount meant you were performing at 100% of quota—acceptable, but not a stellar performance by any means. The amount of bonus generated from meeting a million dollar quota was also rather meager, producing a bonus of about six to eight thousand dollars annually.

However, as sales exceeded quota, the numbers improved substantially. With the additional sales credit I would receive from the new Arthur business, my performance (compared to my quota), would shoot through the roof. Instead of receiving a bonus of ten to twelve grand that year, my bonus would be closer to fifty thousand.

But I didn't deserve it. I had picked up the ball where Mr. Split had left it—at the ten-yard line. I had simply carried it over the goal for the touchdown. But Mr. Split was leaving the company before the bonus payout and would not receive any financial benefit from the new business.

In one of our last conversations before he left the company, Mr. Split recommended I take fifty percent credit for the new business—a more realistic representation of my contribution. I would receive a very nice bonus for my work, and the company would not have to pay the full amount—a fair compromise since the business was un-anticipated and came to me as a windfall.

I suggested this to my manager, explaining my rationalization. He agreed, and complimented me on my "reasonable" approach to the situation, adding that my decision would not only add to the financial benefit received by Acme, I would also be remembered for doing it.

Over the next two months, the first of Arthur Electric's orders began flowing into the system. My next bonus statement showed over fifteen thousand dollars in bonus earnings to date.

Even though I knew I could have received a much higher payout by insisting on full credit, I was happy. I would enjoy a nice financial boost, and I was certain my performance had caught the attention of upper-level management.

I was right. I *was* receiving plenty of attention. But it was all the wrong kind.

The next month, my bonus payout estimate was reduced by half—even though Arthur's business continued to increase. A week later, a revised estimate showed the payout to be a few thousand dollars, and by the end of the month, any bonus consideration from the new Arthur business had been removed from the report.

"Why?" I asked my manager. "What's going on? I didn't think it was possible for the company to manipulate the sales numbers to lower a bonus payout. Is that even legal?"

My manager, let's call him Mr. Robert Doty, didn't try to soften the blow. "The company thinks you and Mr. Split are in collusion, and that you plan to pay him half of your bonus under the table. They don't believe you had anything to do with booking the new business and shouldn't be paid anything. In fact, there are a few people who think you should be fired for trying to misappropriate bonus money that doesn't belong to you."

I went home early that day—unusual for me. Previously, I'd thought nothing of working at my desk until seven pm or coming in on a Saturday for a few hours to catch up on paperwork.

But I knew as I left the office and walked through the parking lot, the days of putting the company first were over. I had just brought the company over a million dollars in new, repeating business, and in exchange, they had branded me a liar and a thief.

I didn't take it lying down. I complained. I asked for an explanation. I pleaded for an opportunity to present my side of the situation. Mr. Split even wrote a letter verifying my participation in negotiating the final numbers and putting the contract together. He added that I was entitled to receive the money and confirmed there were no illegal or unethical arrangements between the two of us. Even the distributor salesman, Danny, called my manager, wanting to know if he could help clear up any confusion about whose efforts were responsible for booking the new business.

My boss called to deliver the final answer. In this case, he was simply the messenger, as the decision originated from his boss, the regional manager (we'll call him Mr. Regional). It was short and to the point. "If Reid doesn't drop this issue, I'll fire him."

"Mr. Regional is a real asshole." I said it out loud.

I couldn't think of a more appropriate response. While my boss didn't respond to my comment, I got the feeling there was a big part of him that agreed with me.

Still not ready to throw in the towel, I asked my manager what he thought about me talking directly to the vice-president of sales. After all, I'd just been tried and convicted without being able to tell my side of the story. And I was damned sure Mr. Regional was enjoying his increased bonus as a result of the new business.

My boss strongly advised me to drop it, especially if I wanted to keep my job.

It was difficult to walk away from a situation that was nothing more than a malicious fiction, created to cast a negative light on my intentions and actions—especially when I was being threatened with termination if I tried to defend myself with the truth. But I knew the regional manager's motivations reflected a personal agenda, and without knowing his end-game, I was at a huge disadvantage.

For every employee that eventually leaves the corporation for greener pastures, there is a turning point, an event or situation that reveals the intolerable truth about the relationship they have with their employer.

This was mine.

Acme had burned the bridge connecting my future with theirs, and they'd left no doubt about who'd struck the match. Discovering that management could give a rat's ass whether I stayed or left was disheartening, and it made me realize it was time to turn my attention to other priorities.

My change in attitude was fueled not only by the arrogance and self-interests of the regional manager but by the discovery that my performance—as measured in dollars and cents—had a limited effect on my compensation. Although there was a supposed correlation in the bonus plan, I'd realized the system was subject to manipulation and was as about as far from a dollar-earned, dollar-shared relationship as you could get. Instead of "paying more for doing more" (management's motivational mantra at the time), my compensation was controlled by two things:

(1) A negatively weighted, inversely proportional formula

(2) The subjective whims of management

And that made the *unofficial* policy very clear: No matter how much business I did, or how much profit I made for the company, my compensation was based on the average amount the company was willing to pay for someone in my position who adequately performed the responsibilities associated with the job. I could only assume this was true regardless of how far up the ladder of management I climbed. And after the Arthur Electric fiasco, I was sure that wouldn't be very far.

There are very few secrets when it comes to employee compensation. Company owners and "purse-string" managers must stay ahead of the game. They take great pains in designing compensation programs to make sure employee income trails productivity. While they may justify this rationale with their "commitment" to a long-term, economically secure relationship (I just heard some of you gag), their real motivation is based on maximizing their return on investment—the one they made in you—and maintaining a specific limit on the amount of company profit they are willing to share with non-owner employees.

Here's the bottom line: Once you've become a regular fixture within the system, management expects you to continue to perform at acceptable levels. Surpassing those levels with exceptional performance will be noticed and perhaps acknowledged, but it will not be recognized as the result of a super-extraordinary effort on your part—because you're a captive asset. You're part of the company, *and it's your job to do everything you can to contribute to its success.* From their perspective, your outstanding achievements are not exceptions, they are what the company hired you to do, and becoming exceptional is an indication of your long term value.

In other words, continue to do outstanding work, and you get to keep your job.

Chapter Five
Your Boss—The Care and Feeding Thereof

In the corporate world, there's not a more critical professional relationship than the one you'll have with your boss. Your immediate supervisor can *and will* make or break your career. You need his or her approval to receive promotions and raises. No other recommendation will carry as much weight.

For the most part, bosses tend to reflect the company's internal values. Otherwise, they wouldn't be in a managerial position. Yes, there are exceptions. Advancement resulting from cronyism and personal relationships is a fact of life. But in general, your boss will reflect a true copy of the company's "big picture," especially when it comes to policy and procedure, and the degree of flexibility you'll have with both.

Have a conflict with your manager's value system? First, determine if it's a personal issue. Does he say or do things that reflect gender bias or discrimination? Are his actions dishonest, deceitful, or ethically flawed? Or is he merely parroting the company's directives and rhetoric? Separate the leader from the system, and decide which one is the real source of the problem.

Bosses come and go, but the core tenets of the company are a perpetual watermark on every expression of its identity. If you find your conflict is with the fundamental principles carved into the bedrock of the organization, you may need to re-evaluate your career future with that company. (To kick it up a notch, if you find you have a constant dislike or conflict will *all* of your bosses, you may not be cut out to be an employee.)

Your first boss can be a valued asset as well as a challenging taskmaster. I've talked with plenty of new hires who expected special consideration in the form of extra patience or even forgiveness from the manager who hired them. And while these "invested" managers can be an excellent source of insight and advice, their expectations for your success will take priority over protecting you with extensions of tolerance or clemency.

A supervisor who had a say in hiring you—or actually made the hiring decision—is under pressure to prove to her superiors she made the right choice. And she will want you to prove her correct as quickly as possible.

From the perspective of senior management, your success is a reflection of your manager's skill and experience in transforming you from a raw trainee into a profitable asset. Every time you screw up or fall short of expected performance goals, or upset or disappoint another employee or customer with inappropriate behavior, someone is silently asking, "Who hired this person?"

Your boss will want to see any personal deficiencies corrected very quickly. The longer you remain with the company as a non-productive employee, the longer a supervisor is reminded that your inadequacies are a reflection of her management skills. You quickly become an on-going embarrassment—a waste of company money and someone who isn't helping to advance their manager's career. If you have difficulty fitting into the organization, or meeting production goals, or exhibiting the traits and characteristics associated with a "good employee," your manager is often the first to issue the ultimatum that eventually results in termination.

Get to know your Boss – really well. The more you know about your supervisor, the more you can influence his thinking. The best approach is to be subtle and non-intrusive. Here are a few suggestions to get you started.

- What are your supervisor's likes and dislikes?

- What's his favorite food or restaurant (so you can suggest it the next time you go to lunch together)?

- Does he attend church? Where? If his actions and behaviors are influenced by adherence to religious principles, how might that affect his expectations about you?

- How long has he been married? Learn his spouse's name. Is he or she a homemaker? Or do they work outside the home? How about the kids? Their names, genders, ages, grades in school, and anything else your boss mentions about them should be committed to memory.

- Find about his hobbies. Does he like sports? Does he attend local events and games? Do his kids play on the school team or in a league?

- What about music? Does he have background music playing in his office? Or does it keep it quiet? Does he play an instrument?

Finally, find out what pisses him off and don't do that. Everyone has hot buttons. Avoid pushing them, and you'll come across as considerate and thoughtful.

There are always a few employees who think it's a show of strength or independence to argue or "raise hell with the boss." It's a mistake. Put yourself in his position and ask yourself how long you would be willing to put up with someone's intentional arrogance when you have a full schedule of responsibilities to complete.

Supervisors look for—and reward—subordinates who make their job easier, who are pleasant to be around, and offer their cooperation and support. If you get the reputation for being a pain in the ass, your future will be a dark one.

These suggestions are just the basics, but it's a start in creating a big-picture of your supervisor's personality, their life priorities, and most importantly, how these may influence their professional decisions.

Do an equal amount of research on your bosses' supervisor. Although you may not have the same access or opportunity for face to face communication, you need to make sure the person with next level authority knows who you are and has a favorable impression of you. Her approval of your boss's recommendation for raises and promotions will be important, if not absolutely necessary. While it may take longer to acquire the same information about regional or national managers, it's vital to your career if your goal is to build your image as a fast-track professional with talents and abilities above and beyond your current position.

Yes, loyalty counts! I'm amazed at the number of people who go behind their supervisor's back to try to have them replaced due to supposed or imagined incompetence, or because they believe they were treated in an inappropriate or unjustified manner, then end up surprised to find out they've committed professional suicide.

Never attempt to undermine your supervisor. The company will not allow it. Your boss is empowered to direct and manage her subordinates, and her superiors will not weaken her authority with wavering or inconsistent validation. To do so would compromise her effectiveness as a manager. Management bestowed your boss with the final decision over your continuing relationship with the company, and whatever your boss decides, the company will support and defend.

While you may personally disagree with your supervisor on policy or procedures, you must find a way to support her decisions and to implement her directions without showing any signs of being disgruntled, resentful, or disappointed.

Above all, avoid having arguments with your boss. In the end, you *will* lose. Unless it's necessary to protect yourself professionally, ethically, or even physically, let your boss have their way.

"But wait!" You say. "What if he's doing something illegal?"

Here's the big question: Are you sure his activities are against the law? Do you have irrefutable evidence that conclusively identifies him as the perpetrator? Keep in mind there's a big difference between doing something illegal and practicing situational ethics.

If your boss *is* operating within the gray zone, and you rat him out, how will it affect your status with the company? A subordinate who challenges a superior's integrity rarely lasts to see another work anniversary. Even worse, there's always the possibility you could be considered complicit in the activity and have the blame shifted to you! Don't underestimate the lengths an organization will go to protect one of their own, especially someone who is a favored son or is owed special consideration from upper management.

Be visible to the boss, but not in her face. The number of opportunities you'll have to converse with your supervisor can vary from an everyday occurrence to once in a blue moon, depending on where she's located. Face-to-face contact may also be determined (limited) by management style, personality, or work schedule. For example, your boss may be more likely to pick up the phone to chat with you about a recently submitted report, even though she's sitting in her office just two doors away.

Despite your supervisor's idiosyncrasies, take advantage of all private meetings. How many meetings? How often? How long?

I've heard management gurus suggest as often as once a week. However, a lot of middle managers are so overloaded with internal paperwork that your request for a weekly meeting could make you a pain in the ass—just the opposite of what you want to accomplish.

Unless your job responsibility requires more frequent face-to-face meetings with your supervisor, shoot for every two weeks. Take cues from your boss's attitude and degree of focus to know when to end the meeting. In general, unless you have something to discuss of biblical proportions, keep the meeting short. Fifteen minutes is usually enough to cover what's going on in your circle of influence. Use the time to update your boss on projects you're working on, trends you've identified, to ask any questions about your performance and promotion opportunities (don't over-do this), and to complement other employees who've helped you or have done something that needs to be acknowledged.

THINK before you speak, then speak without saying, "I think." When your supervisor asks for your opinion, take a moment before answering. If possible, determine the source of the question. Is the information important to her personally, or will it be passed to her superior? Why is *your* input important? Are you being quizzed to determine your progress on an assigned project?

If it concerns company policy, a sales function, or a marketing promotion, dazzle her with suggestions of how you plan to implement the new strategies or procedures. And always avoid prefacing your answer with the words, "I think." It reduces the listener's confidence in your answer because you've expressed an opinion, inferring the source of the information (you!) may not be credible or reliable.

If you can't provide an immediate answer to a question, buy some time. Say you've got some notes, data, or feedback on your computer you'd like to retrieve. Or, you saw an email come in just before the meeting that might have the information you've been waiting on. Then take a few minutes to do some research. If there's a predominant opinion already established within the management hierarchy, and your support of the same view doesn't disadvantage your job or compensation, then you've got your answer.

If a quick round of research doesn't provide you with a response or an opinion you can intelligently promote and defend, return to your boss with this question: "Before we begin, have you had any new thoughts on the situation?" That's all you say. Don't add anything. Then let your supervisor speak. In the few minutes you were gone, his mind has drifted to other things, and it's doubtful he'll think your question is just a ruse to prompt him to disclose his personal opinion. Most of the time, he'll tell you what he thinks and why. Then you can tailor your answer accordingly.

Before we go any further, I want to make it clear I'm not suggesting you need to be a "Yes Man," always responding with the politically correct and diplomatic answer. However, understand this: Communication with your superiors, especially in face-to-face discussions, should be intentionally structured as respectful, professional exchanges in which you exhibit massive doses of self-control.

If you do have verifiable, third-party information contrary to the trending attitude of the company or that contradicts data and information used to justify a management decision, consider the effect your disclosure will have on you and your future. Even when your information is accurate, you could receive a heavy dose of condemnation for bursting the ill-conceived bubble of some misinformed but popular and well-established division head.

Remember, they *do* shoot the messenger, so decide if implicating yourself is the best strategy.

There's another reason to carefully consider revealing any opposing or conflicting information to your manager. If your input criticizes a company plan or program, it can easily be interpreted as an excuse, a reflection of your lack of ability to achieve the results the company wanted. Was the program flawed—or did you fail to perform?

Your commitment and skill in implementation will always be questioned before the viability of the plan or process. So be very careful when expressing a negative opinion about a company campaign or promotion.

If you're tempted to fault the plan because you *are* struggling to achieve an acceptable level of results, explain that your situation is unique because of customer idiosyncrasies, third-party influences, or timing issues, and you're in the process of working through these temporary challenges. You can bet that if you're experiencing negative feedback or outcomes, so are others. Moreover, some of them will be very vocal about it. If a program is truly faulty or ineffective, management will eventually pull the plug.

Keep your conversations with supervisors about *you* and *your* work. Avoid volunteering negative information about co-workers and their activities—both on and off the job. The adage that advises, "If you don't have anything nice to say about someone, don't say anything," is an excellent guideline. Repeating rumor and innuendo about others reflects poorly on your character and professionalism. Even more important, if you acquire the reputation of someone who spills their guts to the boss, you'll lose the respect of your co-workers.

What if the boss asks for private feedback about a co-worker? Yes, this happens. It can come in the form of an off-handed question or after your supervisor provides a detailed disclosure of the issue. And it means one of three things: Your manager is taking you into his confidence and wants to know what you think about another employee. Or, there's a "situation" that involves you and another person—*whether you know it or not*—and he wants to hear your side of the story.

The last alternative typically has to do with a possible promotion, especially if you're competing with another individual for the position. In this situation, questions about a co-worker could be designed to see which of you would make the better supervisor, particularly if one of you is going to end up working for the other.

Regardless of what you believe motivates your supervisor's request for your opinion about another employee, use the following strategy to formulate your answers:

- **Keep your responses general and positive.** Unless you have supervisory responsibility for the co-worker, keep your comments brief and positive. There's never any reason to go into detail about another employee's personal or professional life behind their back. If a pejorative question is asked about a co-worker's job performance, your response should be, "Not that I'm aware of," or "I wasn't aware of that."

- **Be wary of a situation that can put you squarely in the hot seat**: On occasion, you may be asked about a situation or activity that is incriminating to a co-worker or implies their intentions or actions are suspect. If this happens, your answer should always begin—"I've never heard or seen him say or do anything like that." If that's an impossible position to take (because the boss knows for a fact you were aware of what your co-worker was doing), then suggest you didn't think it was your place to bring it up since you had the impression the activity was approved, authorized, or being monitored by management.

In these kinds of situations, saying less is always the best approach, until you know exactly what's going on, and how much management already knows.

Every Boss Has a Personal Management Style.

Management style (sometimes called a *theme*) is a trendy topic and is a popular subject for in-house seminars. Most of these programs suggest replacing a singular communication style with a wider range of methods and techniques to suit the situation or employee. Some of the more common styles are The Director, The Authoritarian, The Coach, and so on. In theory, using multiple management styles will increase a manager's effectiveness, regardless of the differences in personalities between supervisor and subordinate.

Using this form of "flex-management" effectively requires a manager to be constantly aware of what's going on around them, make adjustments based on the intended recipient of their message, and obtain accurate feedback to ensure their ideas and thoughts are accurately interpreted.

Frankly, few people—whether they have management responsibility or not—have the behavioral flexibility to make a seamless transition from one communication style to another. In reality, most managers have an innate management style based on their personality, intelligence, and people skills. And good or bad, it's how they communicate. Although the following categories are generalizations, it's surprising how many subordinates often come to recognize one of these styles as the predictable process of interacting with their boss:

The Questioning Manager. This boss always answers your question with one of his own. If you ask him which product is the better choice for a particular application, he'll answer, "What do *you* think is the better choice? Why don't you spend more time looking over the differences between the two options and see if there's a clear preference?"

Getting a commitment out of a questioning manager is like pulling teeth. Sometimes this style of management is described as an attempt to "soft" delegate, to get subordinates more involved in the process. There's also the possibility you've got someone who's uncomfortable making a decision.

To obtain a definitive answer from this kind of individual, try providing them with a series of logical steps that motivates them to arrive at the conclusion you need. For example, present the choices under consideration, describe the advantages and disadvantages of each, then make a strong recommendation—if you can.

If you can't make a recommendation because you really don't know the best choice, then you're either missing information about the core problem, you're unfamiliar with the relevant details of the situation or affected parties, or it doesn't matter what you decide because the outcome won't make that much difference in the long run. Conversely, if the decision is a foregone conclusion, and your manager's approval is more of an administrative "rubber-stamp," present it that way. "We're ready to implement this, and I just need your signature."

The Waiting/Delaying/Postponing Manager. This manager's favorite mantra is, "I'd rather be right than prompt." Translation: *He's afraid of being wrong.*

Risk is not something a delaying manager wants to calculate, measure, or manage, and he's far more comfortable operating in hindsight than at the forefront. As a result, he seldom gains the advantage of being the first to respond to new opportunities—which, unfortunately, customers may interpret as disinterest.

Your best approach with this kind of manager is similar to the questioning supervisor: Break down your request into phases or steps. Make each step easily explainable in the following terms: (1) Benefits to be gained, (2) Expenses and costs, (3) Estimated return on investment, and (4) Opportunity cost. Tell him you want to take the first step, but that's as far as you want to go until you have obtained positive feedback that you're on the right track, and moving forward makes sense.

Be sure to eliminate all unknown risks from your presentation. Even when they can be evaluated objectively from the three perspectives—worse case, best case, and most likely result—admitting your proposal contains unknown risks will likely generate a response similar to, "Let's hold off on this one until we have a better handle on the situation."

The Re-scheduler. Ask this guy about an unexpected customer meeting or some other unscheduled event, and you're likely to hear, "But that wasn't on the schedule today," or "I didn't realize you would need an answer this soon. You should have brought this to me earlier."

This manager runs his life by day-planner. He couldn't make a spontaneous decision if he had to. Taking him to a restaurant that's different than his regular lunch place can leave him disoriented and confused.

The only way to get something done with this kind of supervisor is to put it on his schedule *first*. If you suddenly need time with him, ask him if he could pencil you in for fifteen minutes that same afternoon, assuring him it's a simple matter that will just take a moment to resolve. The more time you can put between your request and your face-to-face meeting, the more comfortable your manager will be in listening to what you have to say.

You may find it beneficial to schedule a series of mini-meetings throughout the week. This will provide you with pre-arranged time slots to discuss anything that requires his input. If there's nothing urgent when the next meeting rolls around, don't cancel. Instead, review an existing project or situation, then confirm how valuable these brief meetings have been in improving your response time to customers.

The "Not Interested" Manager. If you're suggesting a new system, methodology, or process, you might as well be talking to the cleaning staff. This manager is not interested in changing *anything* unless it comes from above. He expects you to do your job under the existing programs and policies, without finding fault or suggesting improvement. These guys and gals are the metaphorical equivalent of the round peg in the round hole and it couldn't be a more perfect fit. Show them resistance, and you'll leave the room with "Boat-Rocker" stamped on your forehead.

Admittedly, this is a tough one. Fortunately, these types are not without an ego. A *not interested* manager will often consider making a change to the status quo when your suggestion results in accolades for his management skill. The key is using subtle praise to buy more influence. Try increasing your leverage by complimenting him in front of his supervisor. Mention how stable, reliable, and dependable he is. Then add how you appreciate those attributes in someone you work for.

Yes, this kind of brown-nosing can buy you extra consideration, but even when the timing is perfect, always present your request with "negative caution."

Here's an example of some non-threatening rhetoric that neutralizes your personal interest in the subject: "I've been thinking about an alternative way of recording test data from the G-testing we're doing on those new hard-drives. But the more I consider it, the less I'm sure it's even worth discussing. If you'd like, I can run the idea past you. It might be a complete waste of time, but I'd appreciate your input."

Avoid presenting your request in terms of what it will do for you. You'll likely get an automatic turn down. Try saying something like, "I noticed how much paper we were using in copying all those redundant files. I wondered if the company could save a few dollars by printing only what we need from the digital archives. On the flip side, I know there may be other reasons for creating paper copies that I'm not aware of, so I wanted to get your opinion." The fact that you're the one who has to make sure those copies are collated, cross-checked, and filed must not enter into the picture.

The Unpredictable Manager. This guy likes to impress others by leaving no doubt that he's the boss. One of my distributor managers liked to brag he "managed like a bull in a china shop." He prided himself on giving his subordinates as much authority and flexibility as they showed themselves capable of handling, but when he was asked for help or to offer his opinion, he made sure he "got in there and shook things up." He wanted to leave the clear impression he was in charge, and if necessary, would institute silly or unnecessary procedures, just to flex his muscles.

The fact that his reactions were so unpredictable—regardless of what was at stake—motivated his salespeople to avoid asking for his involvement under any circumstances. The thought of their boss communicating directly with customers drained the color from their faces. The same fear was prevalent in the staff as well, and they quickly learned to design their own processes and systems for handling paperwork, correspondence, and other administrative tasks—without asking for input from the boss.

The result? The manager was rarely involved in the day-to-day activities of the business. I don't know if that was his ultimate intention, but it did free up a lot of time to enjoy two-hour lunches and a game of golf twice a week.

Your only defense with a boss like this is to assume a low profile and stay out of his way. These kinds of people typically have huge egos and will go to any length to demonstrate their authority.

Make it a point to avoid disagreements or stating an opposing point of view. If necessary, placate them by agreeing with them in principle, then do what's necessary to get your job done. As far as receiving promotions from an "unpredictable," it will usually help your relationship if you credit him for his management skill and leadership, letting him know it's the very thing that "keeps you on top of your game."

These are just a few of the many management styles commonly identified by personality type or a preferred method of communication. Remember, these are only generalizations. Each manager's style is influenced by their personal agenda, insecurities, and ego. And while some will display a consistent approach to handling their assigned responsibilities, others may pride themselves on their unpredictability.

Chapter Six
Politics and the Power Pyramid

Anyone who dismisses politics as a factor in corporate success is either assuming a posture of self-importance (they're too good to play the game) or they have an erroneous understanding of what the word "politics" really means.

Rooted in Greek culture, politics is the recognition and practice of organizational power and authority, and how that authority is distributed. On a street level, it's about *influence*—motivating others to obtain their support, cooperation, and endorsement.

Knowing how the system works, *and using it correctly*, will give you access to its benefits. Ignoring it, or worse, abusing it, will prevent you from enjoying its advantages.

Your Place in Company Politics . . .

The individual's effectiveness and success within any large workforce are directly related to their recognition, acceptance, and conformity to the company's internal distribution of authority. Translation? You can't expect to be appreciated and valued for your contribution unless you conform to the established and professional "norms" of your company.

And before we go any further, I want to emphasize that this has nothing to do with the draconian and subservient concept of kissing the boss's ass. You can extend professional courtesy and respect without derogating your own feelings of self-worth. While you may not like the idea that all hierarchies come with a chain of authority and a commensurate level of politically motivated behavior, dealing with it isn't optional. Think of it as knowing which piece of silverware to use during a formal dinner, or participating in the rituals of a fraternal organization.

Knowing what to say and how to act within an organized power structure makes you a more valuable part of that structure.

Become familiar with the company's power pyramid. Everyone is familiar with the traditional chart showing a company's hierarchy. At the top is the CEO or president. On the line below, you'll find one or more vice-presidents, defined by division, product line, or geographical authority. On the same level or just below, you'll usually find the chief legal officer, CFO, and other heads of the company. The chart continues to flow down and out, presenting a map of who is responsible for what and who is going to take the blame when things don't go well.

Unless you're promoted or hired for a management level position, your name won't be there. The chart usually stops at the lowest level of management that still includes supervisory responsibility and oversight of multiple employees with common job functions or titles.

Why is the company's hierarchy important? A good barometer for the company's future performance and growth can be found in the personality, management style, and past performance of those located on the upper half of the chart. Simply draw a horizontal line dividing the chart in half. The names on the upper half will determine the destiny of the company.

How much do you know about these "upper-half" managers? Did they work their way up through the organization? Or were they hired-in at a managerial level, and if so, where did they come from?

An internally-promoted manager—the guy or gal who worked their way up from an entry position—will most likely be a dyed-in-the-wool, policy-driven, hymn-singing member of the congregation. They are less likely to be innovators and more likely to tailor their actions and decisions after those of their predecessors.

Know which upper-level managers have a substantial ownership position in the company. Managers at the top of the pyramid, and who also have a significant ownership position can wield power that extends far beyond the authority of their official position. Moreover, their personal level of clout will often take precedence and priority—by default—over the needs of subordinate employees, even when it fails to serve the highest and best interests of the company.

For example, when the manager of one of my distributor accounts was elected president of a national business association, he was invited to our company headquarters to meet Acme's president and to tour several manufacturing plants via the company jet. As the account representative, I was invited to tag along.

After setting a date for the four-day trip, I called our company's PR department and asked the manager to block out the schedule for our exclusive use of the company plane. After reviewing my requested dates, the PR manager said, "You'll have to reschedule. The plane is booked. Mr. Smith (the CEO of Acme *and its majority stockholder)* is using it to attend a ball game in Denver."

In short, he was telling me Mr. Smith's needs took priority over mine—*because Mr. Smith owned the majority interest in the company,* which coincidently, included the plane. It didn't matter that my request was based on satisfying the needs of a customer while Smith's need was strictly personal. As CEO of Acme and the majority stockholder, he was entitled to "owner's privilege," meaning *he gets anything he wants.*

Always make it a point to determine the identity of the owners of the company and their percentages of equity. If a majority stockholder turns out to be one of the company's executive officers, realize that person can wield substantial power. While I'm not suggesting an upper-level manager with a substantial ownership position should be approached in a kneeling position, you should realize their opinion *about you* will carry more clout because of their equity position.

Use the following suggestions to maintain a healthy—and hopefully, reciprocal—level of respect with those in higher positions of authority.

1. **Always show your superiors your best side.** That means displaying a professional persona while in their presence. When senior eyes are on you, you're never off the clock. More than a few careers have been sabotaged by an employee "letting down their hair" at the office Christmas party or having one too many drinks after work. Management needs to know you're the kind of person that stays in control in any environment. Their conclusions concerning your management potential are often based on a simple concept: If you can supervise your own behavior, there's a good chance you can supervise others. Certainly, if the occasion is recreational or social, you should participate and have fun. However, always think of yourself as the guy or gal whom others can turn to if there's a problem because they know you'll have a clear head and will take appropriate and responsible action.

2. **If and when battle lines are drawn, stay neutral.** The best way to stay out of the political crossfire is to avoid the battle completely. Certainly, you'll have an opinion, but keep it to yourself. There are very few times when you *must* declare your support or opposition for a controversial person, program, or policy. If a superior asks for your input, try to determine which way she's leaning. Say something like, "I can see the advantages (merit or benefit) on both sides of the coin. What are your thoughts?" Regardless of your supervisor's answer, respond with, "That makes sense."

The problem with taking sides? Someone ultimately loses. And if you end up on the losing side, the winners may see you as having been shortsighted, mutinous, or disloyal. So to repeat, keep your opinions to yourself. If a co-worker asks you to share your thoughts, defuse the question by saying you're still researching the issue, or you need to learn more about the bigger picture before deciding. You can offer a receptive ear to equals and subordinates who want to tell their story, but avoid outright agreeing—or disagreeing—if possible. A simple "that's interesting. I appreciate you sharing that," will usually placate most gossipmongers and rumor repeaters.

3. **When you find yourself face-to-face with senior management, lock down your mouth and listen!** Having a conversation with an upper-level manager (a ULM) is not an opportunity to demonstrate your ability to "hard-ball it" with the big boys. Avoid the temptation to show off your general business acumen or to impress them with some obscure marketing theory. You'll come across as annoying or pretentious—or both. If a subject comes up in which you are well-versed, *and the manager wants to discuss it,* then yes, dive in. But always obtain their verbal invitation and watch for non-verbal feedback. If you sense you're being placated, immediately stop and ask for their input and opinion.

4. **A phone call from a ULM is not an invitation to chat about the weather or the weekend ballgame.** These folks are busy and have a specific reason for making the call. After a quick exchange of "how are you" and "how is everything going," let the ULM tell you the reason for the call. Answer questions directly without a lot of backstory or history, unless it's something they need to know.

5. **Always go through channels.** Going direct to a higher-level manager without the knowledge and approval of your supervisor is asking for trouble. Although you may have a

personal relationship with a national-level manager, anything having to do with business should always make its way up the chain of command. Intermediate level managers are there for a reason, one of which is to prevent higher-level supervisors from having to deal with questions, requests, and decisions that can be handled by a lesser, more appropriate level of authority.

6. **Never argue or challenge their decisions.** They may (and usually will) have more information about the situation than you. While your concerns will typically focus on how their decisions affect you and your immediate situation, their decisions are often influenced by conditions and circumstances you're not aware of. Moreover, if a personal agenda is involved, you may never know the real reasons for a manager's decision. Your job is to say, "I understand," and follow-up with active indications of your support.

Very important: Any ULM can turn out to be an arrogant idiot or a myopic egotist, or both. However, never throw down the gauntlet in front of them. The more they believe you're on their side, the more consideration you'll receive in the future. He or she may be your enemy, but they must never know it, especially if you're going to rise to a management level equal to theirs—and beyond.

7. **Always show your support for your immediate supervisor.** It doesn't matter if it's during a one-on-one, private conversation with a ULM or while in the presence of others, never undermine, criticize, or say anything negative about your boss. If a senior manager says something derogatory about your supervisor, decline his invitation to support it. He may be baiting you. Until you know the intent of the accusation— whether stated or implied— avoid saying anything you'll wish you could retract later. If a ULM presses you for an opinion, offer positive generalities. For example, "She's been very

helpful. My experience with her has been good. I hope this is just a minor glitch for her."

Corporate politics, as maligned and one-sided as they often are, reflects a combination of personalities, power issues, and personal agendas. And like any other organized groups with a common mission—including your local book club, fraternal organization, and the church you attend—there's nothing so unusual about the corporate version of politics to make it substantially different from the social dynamic operating within any other formal association of people.

With one exception . . . *It's the source of your livelihood.*

While you may decide to walk out of your neighborhood HOA meeting to protest the president's preference to use his brother-in-law's landscaping company, your actions in response to your employer's politics must be tempered with a different priority.

Chapter Seven
The Importance of Corporate Culture and It's Influence on Your Career

"In a company with a great culture, the backstabbing only produces a flesh wound." – Roger A. Reid

Defining organizational culture is like trying to describe all the patterns and variations of color in a kaleidoscope. Not only will the descriptions vary by individual, the significance and meaning of what they see will also differ. For example, some might find the colors soothing and a welcome break from what they were doing. Others will think it's a silly waste of time.

It's the same with culture. While most of us can describe the idea of culture in broader terms—using phrases like, "that's the way we do things around here," or "it's the way we act and interact with each other"—attempting to pinpoint *exactly* what culture means to the employee tends to generate as many different answers as you have people contributing an opinion.

For some, it's the environment and work style, with perks like a park-like campus, unstructured work areas, flexible hours, and a lunch cafeteria offering ten flavors of yogurt. Others set their priorities on the intellectual competence of their co-workers and the opportunity for advancement into management.

Why such a difference in our individual perceptions of culture? Because over the last two decades, the cultural ideal has evolved from an often nebulous set of "higher values" and principled standards to tangible, value-added advantages for the employee. In short, what was traditionally expressed in paragraphs of flowing rhetoric—usually a vague description of the company's ethical responsibility to "do the right thing"—has been transformed into tangible benefits, often including an employee-centered environment where comfort, convenience, and activities designed to meet personal needs are integral to the workplace.

This transition has accelerated over the last decade, especially with millennials moving into positions of upper management in the workforce. As a result, a company's culture has become fundamental to its identity. It's not unusual for college seniors to evaluate a potential employer solely on its culture: "I think Company A has a better culture, so that's the one I want to work for." Or, "You wouldn't catch me talking to anyone from company B. Its culture sucks."

This "New World" concept of organizational culture is becoming such a commonly used yardstick to measure a company's environmental, physical, and intellectual benefits, that even the most every-day and commonplace features of a company's landscape are often interpreted as intentional expressions of culture. In this context, culture can mean anything from covered parking spaces to casual Friday.

The result? As our perception of work culture shifts more toward an expression of tangible benefits, the idea of creating a positive, productive workplace becomes less about a sacred mantra of principles, vision, and values, and more about campus gyms, on-site daycare, and a staff nurse handing out vitamin C pills during cold and flu season.

And that's dangerous.

With cost-intensive benefits masquerading as cultural imperatives, the waters of entitlement have gone from murky to muddy. Especially since the growing pool of "desirable conveniences" are commonly, yet mistakenly used as metrics to measure the presence, effectiveness, and value of a company's culture.

The truth?

When the money is flowing and profits are up, culture—under our New World definition— is a many-faceted reflection of the bottom line. Unfortunately, that's also true when the intersecting lines on the whiteboard show profits plummeting through the floor.

This makes profits and culture—when measured as tangible, value-added employee benefits—not only interrelated but lock-stepped in co-dependency. Make no mistake: It's money first, culture second—ALWAYS. If you doubt the priority, try rating the culture behind the locked doors of an abandoned manufacturing plant.

Let's look at a real-world example. Why does Google have a much-envied work environment that continually puts the company on everyone's list of top places to work? Because Google makes lots of money. Their income is presumably in excess of what is required to pay the ongoing cost of payroll and salary, debt service, research and development, physical plant maintenance and replacement, employee benefit packages, upper management perks, and stockholder dividends.

So when given the choice of whether to pay taxes on windfall profits or use tax-deductible funds to the symbiotic benefit of employees, in the words of the most conservative accountant, "Why not?"

As long as the money continues to flow, life is good.

However, things can change. Markets crash. Customers can lose their financial ability to purchase your products or services. The competition can reverse-engineer a company's core product and duplicate it for a tenth of the cost. And for the sake of the organization—for its survival—the hard influences of financial continuity must take priority over the softer aspects of culture. The result? All those nice benefits previously delivered under the guise of "culture" must be curtailed.

The concept is about as straightforward as it gets—the company must cut non-essential spending due to a drop in income, profit, or both. And yet, employees often feel betrayed and even resentful when value-added benefits are lost due to the *hard* realities of reduced cash flow, industry downturns, and a hundred other situations that can affect the company's bottom line.

Under the New World definition of culture, employees must understand how the realities of business can affect their jobs and future security. They should realize the company isn't bulletproof and needs their support and dedication to thrive economically through both good and lean times.

If you've been following me so far, you should be getting the idea that a healthy culture is a two-way street. Ideally, it promotes or provides *personally-valued benefits* to the majority of employees. In exchange, the company expects to profit from increased employee productivity, loyalty, and engagement. Which brings us to the sobering conclusion that the more the company's culture is measured in the form of tangible benefits, the more the culture is dependent upon the financial success of the company.

Here are six fundamental truths about company culture:

1. **The concept of organizational culture is in transition.** Previous definitions of culture usually focused on three primary areas:

(a) The way—the how, when, and where—the majority of employees do their job, especially when responding to a customer request or problem.

(b) The methods of management—how many levels, how much authority, and the quality and consistency of communication (often the degree of transparency) between management and their subordinates.

(c) The level of employee empowerment, and how an individual's responsibility compares to their authority to get the job done well and on time.

And while those descriptions are still accurate, a new and younger generation of workers is expanding that definition to include tangible benefits that directly affect the employee's experience in the workplace. As this transition continues, this "New World" definition—and the expectations it creates in the minds of employees—will make the tangible extensions of culture more dependent on the company's financial bottom line.

2. **Every company has a culture**. A lingering point of confusion is that a company must formally institute a cultural agenda, or at least define what their culture is—otherwise, it doesn't exist. But in reality, every business has a culture. If it isn't formalized, or defined by policy, example, or from the expectations of management, *then it exists by default*. It may be good, bad, or downright toxic, but make no mistake, every business has a culture.

3. **Culture—whether it manifests itself in psychic or material benefits—is, ultimately, an expression of profit.** Nothing more and nothing less. It takes its form and longevity from the business activity that allows it to exist. When profits are on the rise, a company's culture typically expands, creating a more tangibly apparent, benefit-enriched environment. Conversely, when business is in decline, culture must contract, eliminating financially-prohibitive actions and benefits while management becomes less flexible in evaluating and satisfying employee-centered expectations.

4. **A cultural statement containing words like "beliefs, values, and principles" is suspect at best.** Unifying the belief systems of a diverse workforce carries a degree of difficulty

similar to walking on water. In its most practical incarnation, it can influence recruitment (attracting people of a similar mindset), but even with the best of intentions, a "like-minded hiring policy" is far too subjective to be useful, and in a worse case situation, can be misinterpreted (or manipulated) to be an infringement on a protected class.

In reality, corporations have objectives, goals, and plans. If beliefs and values are going to enter the picture, they will originate from the company's owners and board of directors, who are influenced by personal agenda, financial goals, and traditional industry practices. These inputs may determine the "scheme of things" *at that point in time.* The results are decisions and policies that affect the work environment and influence how employees and customers perceive the company—*until they change.*

5. **Realize that authentic transparency is a fantasy and is rarely (if ever) practiced voluntarily.** Revealing the hard truths of intention, motivation, and purpose is counterintuitive to the mindset of upper-level management. Their rarefied world has always contained privileged secrets. For example, maintaining the financial well-being of the stockholders may be an obvious company responsibility, but revealing its priority to be higher than furnishing employees with free coffee and pastry every morning may not sit well with the rank and file. Consequently, if the company's real objective is to line the pockets of the CEO and her lieutenants, it's doubtful you'll find that disclosed as a priority in the company's cultural statement. The greater the difference between the private intentions of management and the company's "official" objectives, the greater the likelihood of increased employee doubt, suspicion, and an "us versus them" mentality, especially when the company promotes an employee-centered philosophy while the day-to-day reality still reflects business as usual.

6. **An organization's existing culture**—regardless of the form it takes—cannot be used as an imperative standard by which to make assumptions about the company's future relationship with its employees. Even objectively-measured incentives are subject to change. A downturn in the market or the bottom line can transform the friendly, smiling recruiter who welcomed you with open arms into a snarling, flesh-eating ogre who's knee-deep in carnage from previously terminated co-workers.

Use the concept of "culture" to your benefit, regardless of whether you're a Loyalist or a User. Now that we know more about what culture is (and what it isn't), we can talk about how to use the concept to your personal benefit.

First, if your company has created a formal statement of organizational culture, read every word of it. Become familiar with it to the point that you can discuss the general theme in detail. You may even want to memorize the main headings. Being able to quote the highlights is impressive, and it shows you've not only taken an interest in the operational values and expectations of the company, but you also genuinely care about incorporating them into your work activities—giant gold stars for those on their way up.

In addition, if you're ever asked to provide feedback on your company's culture, or find yourself discussing the subject with management, consider using the following talking points. They'll get you remembered as someone who understands the delicate balance between manifesting culture in a tangible form and the difficulties in budgeting long-term benefits in a volatile, competitive marketplace:

- **Avoid adopting a *Me Too* approach to meet the "standards and values" of other companies in the same industry.** With all the attention and focus on culture, there's a temptation to change, update, streamline, humanize, or otherwise transform a company's culture to align with popular trends—*to be one of the good guys.* This kind of motivation often results in poster-worthy phases describing an ideal workplace, but not much more. Instituting cultural change is an inside job, not a knee-jerk response to outside pressures. If management is serious about enhancing their employee's environment or improving the work experience, the process is no different from making any other kind of improvement or asset purchase. First, determine the cost (in dollars, time, and disruption to the existing environment and protocol), and the impact, if any, on other company programs. Then prioritize the benefits based on the cost of acquisition, the percentage of employees who would take advantage of them, and the calculated return on investment measured in objective terms (less sick days, employee retention, higher quality new hires, etc.).

- **Employees should be made aware of their responsibility for the on-going expense of a benefit-rich work environment.** By realizing that tangible benefits come with a cost that is directly affected by profitability, it's easier to rationalize the need to produce additional, offsetting gains in productivity. As a result, workers are more likely to recognize and appreciate workplace advantages that are otherwise taken for granted.

- **Keep it simple.** A thirty-thousand-word dissertation on situational ethics and their application in the workplace is a throwback to someone's Master's thesis. If you need a multi-level table of contents, glossary, or a dictionary to understand it, it's doubtful the principles and concepts will ever manifest themselves into day-to-day operations. The best implementations of culture are simply stated and easily demonstrated. That means specific and measurable methods of how culture will take practical shape and form.

- **Keep it realistic.** If it's not transferable into recognizable demonstrations of "doing something better," it's just theory. Fantasized culture wastes time and creates doubt in the minds of employees. Be able to point to concrete evidence of your "culture" at work. Give it a real presence. Maybe it *does* manifest itself in covered parking and free coffee. If so, make sure the employees know about it. A philosophical treatise describing the ideals of "working together to build a better tomorrow" is bullshit, especially if it doesn't result in something discernible in the everyday work lives of the employees. It may take the form of recognizing workers for their dedication, loyalty, and consistently meeting team and organizational goals, or it might mean scrubbing the names from the reserved parking places of upper management to remove the perception of narcissistic elitism. To be effective, culture MUST make lives better, easier, or provide something the employee can point to and say, "My company does this, or provides that, and I think it's great." Those are the kind of accolades that give culture presence and value.

- **Build internal culture from external financial success.** Every company wants the marketplace to think of them as the good guys—people who care about their customers and demonstrate it with value, excellent customer service, and ethical interaction with the environment and society in general. In short, people want to buy from companies that leave a positive footprint. The benefits are obvious: Retention of customers as measured in repeat business, attracting top talent from the job market, and retaining good employees because they enjoy being part of something they're proud of. Work on this external component first and internal culture can evolve organically—because the financial success required to support it will be in place.

What do you say when asked for your opinion on culture? It might happen during a review, or over lunch with a visiting division head. The topic is usually introduced when an upper-level manager says something like, "The evolving cultural influences in the current business environment tells us we need to begin placing a definite emphasis on responding to the needs of the employee."

If you're expected to comment, I suggest using the paragraph below word for word. It's the kind of rhetoric managers love to hear. In fact, it may be what they *need* to hear to recommend you for advancement. It says you understand the concept and the relationships between sales, expenses, and profit—the holy trinity of business.

"Organizational culture is an extension of economic feasibility. No company can provide what it cannot afford—at least not in the long run. And as our concept of culture expands to meet the needs of a changing workforce, we must find ways to create a realistic and manageable balance between cost, employee satisfaction, and the future financial growth of the company."

Chapter Eight
Draw a Line Between Your Personal and Business Life (and Keep it Flexible)

This can be one of the most daunting challenges of successfully negotiating the corporate bureaucracy. If you've been recognized as someone with management potential or have exhibited other "high-profile" aptitudes, your managers will expect you (and often your spouse) to participate in all company-sponsored events, including those that appear to be primarily social. If you're already on the management fast-track, your responsibility for "presence" will correspondingly expand to make you even more visible.

Since we've touched on the subject of spouses, let's talk about the importance of your marital status and how it can affect your career path.

Married or single—does it matter?

The term *"glass ceiling"* has been used for decades to describe the virtual barrier that prevents certain classes—women and minorities in particular —from advancing into higher levels of management. Yes, it still exists, and the bias, prejudice, and erroneous preconceptions that perpetuate it often include marital status.

Here's the short answer: When it comes to married versus unmarried employees, with all other factors equal, the married employee will receive more points for stability and consistent emotional balance. Here's why: A single guy or gal poses a lot of "what if" questions. What if he or she meets someone who lives out of town and decides to move to be with them? What if a love affair ends on a sour note and leaves one or both of the employees emotionally devastated, impacting their performance?

Call it flawed logic or irrational speculation, but a married person is a known entity, and managers usually assume a married candidate's future to be less subject to personal situations that could be detrimental to the company.

Am I suggesting that, for the sake of their careers, singles find partners and tie the knot as quickly as possible? No, just be aware of the "tainted single" prejudicial attitude that can influence management's evaluation of your future potential.

If you're currently without a significant other, you can neutralize some of the perceived instability of your "singleness" by keeping your sexual exploits to yourself. Yes, I mention this in another chapter, but it's important enough to repeat: If someone asks you how you spent your weekend, keep your responses vague, with references that indicate you're a home-body. If pressed for details, tell others that most of your free time is spent taking online courses, working out at the gym, or pursuing some aspect of self-improvement. You may be dying to brag about the threesome you had Saturday night, but in a word—don't.

If you're attending a corporate-sponsored event where other employees will be accompanied by their spouses or partners, consider asking a friend to go with you. Make sure to choose someone who knows how to behave themselves in a professional setting, can chat up a storm, and knows how to turn on the charm. (I know, if you'd found someone like that, you'd have married them. Just do the best you can, keeping in mind that it's better to go alone than with someone who drinks too much, or whose personality leaves others feeling placated or insulted.)

Romantic relationships between employees.

For decades, companies have used behavioral guidelines, environmental influences, and formal policies to keep their employees from engaging in flirtation, romance, and sex.

Human resource departments continue to hire independent consultants to present workshops on curtailing sexual overtures and innuendo. Periodic memos are constantly circulated to remind employees to keep explicit conversations, public displays of affection, and sexual overtures outside the office.

Has it worked? It depends on how you measure it. I think the level of casual flirtation is probably about the same. Even when companies institute new policies to control or eliminate it, the resulting atmosphere only *appears* less affected. As most will tell you, it's still there, bubbling just under the surface.

Thankfully, here's what *has* changed . . .

The blatant, historically male-initiated sexual overtures—especially when delivered with intimidating and inferred ultimatums—are pretty much a thing of the past. Victims now have voice and recourse, and offenders are no longer protected by their job status or value to the company.

That being said, people working for the same company still meet, become attracted to each other, and end up having consensual sex. Some fall in love and get married. Others fall in love, get divorced, and then get married.

Here's the big question: If tempted, what do you do?

First, consider your company's rules and policies concerning an inter-office romance. Assuming there are strict directives for acceptable employee behavior while on company time and property, it's also a good bet that repeated infractions can result in automatic termination—for at least one of you. However, if you're determined to ask out that cute brunette in accounting—despite the risk to your career—here are some guidelines:

Be discrete. Don't ask a co-worker out while you're within earshot of someone else. It can be embarrassing for both of you. When asking, don't gush about your pent-up feelings or use language that should be reserved for the bedroom. Simply ask the question: "Would you like to go to . . . ?"

If you're turned down, don't ask twice. It's not only rude; it could also be considered harassment. Even though you deliver your second invitation with courtesy and respect, if the recipient of your interest becomes uncomfortable, you've crossed the line, and you can be held accountable for it.

Keep sex off the table during the first date. Make your first date a casual lunch or a cup of coffee after work. If all goes well and you both decide to indulge, explore the possibilities OUTSIDE of company time and property. Taking the secretary out to the parking lot for a "noon-er" in the backseat of your Chevy will not be appreciated by management, and if your sex partner du jour regrets the activity later, your lack of judgment WILL come back to haunt you.

Keep the relationship to yourself. Don't share the fact that you're dating a company employee. Make sure your partner understands the need for secrecy as well. Most companies consider romantic activity between employees an unwanted distraction within the workplace, affecting not only the two people involved but others who know about it. If it negatively influences office productivity, one or both of you may find yourself being transferred or terminated.

Agree on rules of disengagement before things get serious. If it doesn't work out—and most of the time, it won't—have a mutually acceptable understanding of how to break up or at least wind things down. Think of it as a dating prenuptial. If your relationship grows and you end up together in the long term, great. If not, you'll have some rules to help normalize your post-breakup behavior at work. Remember, if one of you loses interest and calls it off, you'll still have to work together. And that can be a big order. Here are a couple of suggestions to include in your pre-relationship discussion:

1. Agree that if either party decides to call it quits, they must be honest and disclose their feelings as soon as possible.

2. Neither of you are allowed to suddenly stop calling or radically change your behavior toward the other without a full explanation of what's going on. Not knowing *why* a relationship ends only adds to the hurt and disorientation of rejection. Being honest can also help reduce the animosity and outright hostility the injured party can feel toward the other.

The mid-twentieth century adage of "Don't stick your pen into the company inkwell," was an early attempt to warn employees (primarily men) to consider their co-workers in the same way as they would any company asset—don't abuse it, never exploit it, and don't even think about taking it home. And yet, many couples can still remember the first time they laid eyes on their spouse—riding together in the same elevator, chatting in the company lunchroom, or sitting next to each other at a business conference—brought together because they were employees of the same company.

I must admit to having a special affinity for this group of love-struck co-workers since I, too, married a co-worker. And after 25 years of marriage, I consider our meeting, relationship, and resulting marriage to be the most positive and influential event in my life. Just because you both happen to work under the same roof should not be a reason to eliminate each other as a possible life partner. Just remember, an office romance has a much greater—*and safer*—chance of longevity when passion is moderated with equal does of caution, discretion, and responsible judgment.

Vacations and taking time off work

I could cite all kinds of studies that show the advantages of taking vacations. However, the following story does a much better job at making my point:

After ten years at Acme, I'd earned three weeks of vacation, but as December rolled around, I had not taken a single day off. That particular year had been especially hectic. One of our sales engineers had been transferred to another office, leaving us shorthanded. And after six months, his replacement was still a couple of months away. As a result, my inside sales assistant, Jill, and I took over his customers, including all associated order administration and follow-up.

Taking a vacation that year was simply not an option. In the most literal sense, taking time off work would have damaged the company's relationship with dozens of customers, cost hundreds of thousands of dollars in lost business, and put an unacceptable workload on my assistant—something I refused to do.

As I looked at my planning calendar to determine the days our office would close for the December holidays, I realized I had enough vacation days to take the entire month of December off—an impossible fantasy.

I mentioned this to my boss who responded by acknowledging my loyalty to the company and then added he would ask the regional manager—who was in the office that day—to approve additional compensation equal to a month's salary, financially offsetting my forfeited vacation time. In his mind, there was no question I had given up my vacation due to company circumstances, and more importantly, the company had benefited from it.

Believing Mr. Regional would approve the request, my supervisor posed the question to him while the three of us were in the same room.

Mr. Regional got a bothered look on his face and mumbled, "That's not possible." Directing his comments at me, he added, "You should take your vacation days when they're available.

Giving them up is a personal decision, and the company can't be responsible for poor planning on your part."

Until that day, I'd never realized how far a person could put their head up their ass. This guy recognized value only when it was of benefit to him. Since he didn't see how pulling several thousand dollars out of his discretionary account would be of any immediate advantage to him *personally*, he attacked my well-intentioned efforts with criticism.

So that year I gave the company an extra three weeks of uncompensated work. Double work in fact—my own and, with Jill's help, that of the missing salesperson. I also learned how much the company valued and appreciated my sacrifice, in dollars and cents—terms we both understood.

But wait! Isn't it possible to hurt your career by taking vacations? There are a surprising number of employees who allow a large percentage of their vacation days to go unused every year. They typically cite the following reasons:

- Their workload is too heavy to leave

- There's too much going on at work right now

- The timing isn't right

- The fear that being gone too long—typically more than a week—could hurt their chances for promotion.

If you're worried that your absence will negatively impact your career, express your concerns to your supervisor. Explain that you want to make sure your vacation doesn't impose undue stress on others or cost the company new business. This should be done during a private meeting after you've prepared the following:

1. List any contracts, meetings, correspondence, or other communication scheduled for completion or expected by others during your absence. Explain that you have rescheduled the

non-critical items and will complete the high-priority work prior to your leaving. How do you identify a high-priority task? If it's something that needs to come from you to ensure its accuracy, or will result in a bottom line you'll have to live with (performance goals, for example), bite the bullet, and get it done before you leave.

2. Make arrangements with a co-worker to take over any direct customer responsibility you may have. When someone calls for you while you're out of the office, make sure the person responsible for answering the phone knows to route your calls to the substitute. (Obviously, you'll offer to return the favor when the situation is reversed.)

3. If you feel it's necessary—either to placate your boss or to demonstrate the importance you place on your job—provide your travel itinerary and contact information. It's usually a good idea to suggest the perceived level of need before others interrupt your vacation. In other words, is it okay to call to get your opinion on a situation that could have waited until you returned? Or do you want to be interrupted only for critical questions and decisions that could cost the company (and you) money? Also make sure your boss knows your preference for contact (phone, email, text).

Associations with fraternal and professional organizations.

Unless there is a definite advantage in disclosing your association with a fraternal or professional organization (for example, because your supervisor or a member of senior management is also a member), you're better off not mentioning it.

Even though the purpose and intent of many fraternal groups are primarily altruistic, the majority of companies will consider your affiliation with any club, charity, alliance, or organized group as a distraction.

Management wants you to spend your productive efforts exclusively on their behalf. Revealing your association with a fraternal organization may cause a supervisor to wonder if . . .

• While you're at work, are you distracted by the bake sale you're organizing that weekend at the Elks Lodge?

• How often will your responsibilities as a Mason take priority over your job?

• Are you using company time and resources to make phone calls, produce copies for members, or sort your mailing list on behalf of fraternal organizations?

The only reasonably safe exception? Church. Any organization having a religious connotation is usually hands-off. One reason is that most services and meetings take place on Sunday, a day that doesn't exist on the corporate calendar. If you attend services on Saturday or help out with church-sponsored activities, you can usually get away with it, but keep in mind you'll still be expected to give up the occasional weekend when company travel is required.

As a salaried employee, the company will fail to see a hard line between personal and business time. And as you move up the ranks into upper management, you'll find that line increasingly blurred. For example, if your goal is to rise to a division manager or vice-presidency, you'll need to project the persona of a "company man," someone who is never off the clock, and always available to pursue the interests of the organization.

Dealing with an unwanted promotion or a request to move to another location.

Being forced to deal with an unwanted offer of promotion or a new assignment that requires relocation can be a double-edged sword. Turning down a promotion—even if your reasons are justified—can create serious doubts about your commitment to the company's objectives and priorities.

Relocations can be especially damaging to Users. For example, if your long-term career plans are based on the eventual creation of your own business, a move half-way across the country can be disruptive and may delay the launch date of your personal venture by months or even years. This is particularly true if you're planning on using your local base of contacts to help grow your business after you leave the corporation.

It's a thin line, and it gets thinner over time. You may be able to turn down the first or even the second offer of relocation, but a third refusal will establish a pattern, and your long-term value to the company will come into question. I know plenty of Users whose third offer came with an ultimatum: Accept the new assignment or seek other employment.

This may seem like the corporate version of cutting off their nose to spite their face, but it's an extremely common ploy to separate the Users from the Loyalists. I've personally experienced it twice.

The first time occurred when I was employed by Mountain Bell (Yep, the old phone company) and after working for a year, I was offered a transfer to Phoenix, Arizona. Currently assigned to the Mountain Bell office in Yuma, I'd taken the job after completing my second year in college. Since my real intention was to work a couple of years to save enough money to return to school and complete an engineering degree, a move to Phoenix made no sense. My living expenses would be much higher, the job would require more drive time, and as a result, building my savings would take much longer. In short, I saw the move as counter-productive to accomplishing my real goal of returning to college to complete my degree.

I turned it down.

Mountain Bell's response? "We have nothing else for you."

At the time, their decision infuriated me. I'd believed their offer was presented as an opportunity for advancement, not a contingency for continued employment. But the regional manager was an egotistical hot-head. He interpreted my refusal to move as an insult, a personal affront to his authority, and I was summarily punished for it. (Yes, I quit the phone company and went back to school a year earlier than planned, paying the bills with part-time jobs and student loans.)

The second time I received a "career ultimatum" was during my fourteenth year with the "Acme" corporation. The offer of relocation came raw and unwrapped, without promises or accolades, and missing all the earmarks of a reward for a job well done.

At the time, I was working in the Phoenix office and had just been assigned a new manager resulting from a company-wide reorganization. My newly ordained boss immediately decided I would be more useful in Denver. I asked my new boss, "What happens if I turn it down?" The manager's answer was swift and simple: "You can seek other employment."

Here's the point: An offer of promotion or relocation can serve many purposes, *all* of which will be in the best interests of the company. Whether or not you share in any of those benefits will be based on your ultimate end game—what you want to accomplish in the next five to ten years of your life.

If your current position is as far as you're willing to go with your current employer, your best defense against unwanted relocation is to create a situation "outside your control" that explains why you can't—as opposed to won't—accept a promotion or relocation. Here are a few that have been used successfully to rationalize a refusal to move:

- **A health condition**. Never yours, but affecting a family member. (Compromised personal health is a liability that could put you on the shortlist for termination.) This could be in the form of a well-documented allergy to the plant life or environmental pollution in the new location, or a family member who cannot tolerate the heat, cold, humidity, or altitude. It will add credibility to your story by referring to these symptoms as inducers of more serious problems, such as circulatory issues, asthma, shortness of breath, vertigo, stroke, etc.

- **The lack of educational facilities at the new location, especially if you're continuing your education under company supervision or sponsorship**. I mention this but don't bank on it. In the past, making a move before finishing an advanced degree could put its completion at risk. Now, that's seldom the case. Online courses, extension classes, and other at-a-distance options are commonplace, and the need for physical presence in a classroom has been eliminated. A stronger argument, however, can often be built on a child's need to remain in their current school, as explained below.

- **Children.** This is probably the most powerful defense against relocation, especially in the middle of a school year. There's plenty of data that can easily be manipulated to show the detrimental effects of uprooting a child during a school year. Portraying your decision to turn down a transfer because you must default to the higher priority of being a good father or mother will generally be received as commendable. But remember, your refusal to move may still result in termination, but you'll leave with the admiration of your co-workers.

- **The potential loss of your spouse's job.** Always express this as a secondary concern to your own career. Never give the impression your spouse's job is of higher priority than yours. As far as the company is concerned, *your job is the one that counts* and should always be given precedence over the income-generating activities of other family members. If it becomes a conflict, the company will eventually ask you to choose between your spouse's career and your own, especially if they are grooming you for a managerial position.

- **Religious ties to a church or congregation.** Be very careful with this one. A manager once confided in me that his decision to terminate a salesman—a devout Mormon—was based on the employee's lack of productivity. The employee saw it differently. He believed his firing was due to his refusal to move from Salt Lake City. The truth? The guy was doing a lousy job, but he might have received a second chance if he'd accepted relocation to a larger office where he could have received more supervision. The takeaway? Rationalizing a need to stay put for religious reasons loses all merit if you're not performing at an acceptable level.

Remember, none of these reasons is a guaranteed ticket out of relocation, but they can motivate a human resource manager to take a second look at company liability in the event your firing could result in a wrongful termination suit.

Chapter Nine
Looking Out For Number One

In this section, we're going to talk about professional self-defense for your career, including the best ways to stay under HR's radar and avoid being targeted for termination.

Your workday should always be executed with a precautionary mindset designed to protect your professional reputation, a vital component to your long term success.

Beware Human Resources – Department of Smoke and Mirrors. Its name—Human Resources—suggests a division of the company dedicated to the well-being and advancement of the company's employees. It sounds like a downright friendly and inviting place, where you can find the help you need to accelerate your career, work through problems, and increase the enjoyment and satisfaction you receive from your work. The term *human resources* conveys such a sense of positivity about it, it's easy to assume the HR department to be a place designed to serve and benefit the company's workforce.

Right?

In a word . . . wrong.

In three words . . . wrong, wrong, wrong.

If I could suggest a new name that more accurately describes what goes on inside the HR department, I'd offer this: "Department for the mitigation of corporate liability in managing employee discipline, exits, terminations, and transfers."

The HR department's number one responsibility is to protect the company from liability. The primary source of this liability originates from wrongful termination lawsuits and damage claims resulting from alleged discrimination or harassment. Notice the emphasis on *protecting* the company. The HR department represents the company's interests and assets, not yours.

In short, the HR department *IS* the company, pared down to its most legal and protective persona. When you talk to anyone in HR, consider your conversation—your choice of subject and what you choose to reveal—the same way you would if speaking to a lawyer for the opposing side.

Santa isn't the only one with a naughty list. In addition to mitigating liability resulting from employee interactions and terminations, HR also keeps a watchful eye on employee behavior, hoping to ferret out potential problems and eliminate the "bad apples" in the earliest stages. Their tools are managing to terminate (managing out), demotion, transfers, and large-scale employee termination via lay-offs and downsizing.

HR is the quintessential incarnation of the wolf in sheep's clothing. More than one HR manager has revealed how naive most employees are about the department's function, with most workers never realizing HR's intentions are seldom—if ever—in the best interests of the individual worker.

One ex-HR manager once related the subtle irony of the department's typical smoke and mirror approach by recalling HR's presentation of an in-house motivational seminar designed to promote sensitivity and tolerance between co-workers on the same day they circulated a memo to management, titled, "Make sure the discharge is legal."

"But I'm the model employee," you say. "I have nothing to fear from HR."

Even the best employees can find themselves suddenly engaged in a conversation with HR due to a takeover, buyout, or reorganization. So never let your defenses down. Unless you originate the correspondence, treat any communication from HR as a threat to terminate, even when disguised as an opportunity to transfer, acquire more education, or the possibility of a promotion. Be courteous, professional, and prompt. And never give them a reason to doubt your loyalty.

How can you stay on the good side of HR? By avoiding the most egregious "sins" cited by HR managers as "actionable offenses requiring intervention." You may want to use the following suggestions to create a personal behavior code that defines your line in the sand—one you must never cross. Exceptions are seldom—if ever—justified by the situation, the circumstances, or the aberrant behavior of others. So consider these to be "fatal errors," with little chance of forgiveness.

1. **Never threaten anyone**, either with idle intent or physical violence.

2. **Never badmouth the company in the presence of others.** That includes expressing dissatisfaction with your job, compensation, your supervisor, or company policy. Keep in mind there is no such thing as a "private conversation" on company property. Ears are everywhere, and there's always a chance someone will overhear you. If you need to vent, buy a diary and fill it with a daily record of gripes, complaints, and grievances. Remember to keep it locked away at home so no one else can read it.

3. **Stay cool and collected under fire.** While you may think you're occasionally entitled to curse, vent, or blow off steam, the results can and will hurt you. Just because the conversation turns heated or you're put under pressure, there's no excuse for verbal attacks and derogatory statements—even when they're true. Going ballistic may seem like the only option you've got, but others will see your emotional outburst as a symptom of fear and emotional immaturity. Even worse, it's an indication that the other guy got to you, and you couldn't handle it. Make it a habit of silently dismissing the stupid behavior and comments of others. It demonstrates you're

operating on a much higher level, and in fact, have the capacity to handle far more serious situations.

4. **Avoid making negative comments or innuendo about another employee.** Although similar to misdeed number two, expressing negativity about others is so prevalent in the workplace, it deserves more emphasis. Never trash a co-worker, not even to a trusted confidant. The moment it leaves your lips, it's out there—a loose missile no longer under your control—and you never know when it's going to circle back and blow up in your face. By keeping negative comments out of your conversations, you'll be safeguarding your reputation and character. Regardless of how poorly another employee is doing, never volunteer a negative opinion about them. If you have responsibility for their performance, and your manager pushes you to deliver a less than glowing evaluation, do it with a positive spin, indicating that with more direct supervision, feedback, or directed assignments there's a chance for improvement.

5. **Avoid becoming a company liability**. This is why the HR Department is continually pumping out all those little signs and posters warning workers to avoid the possession and use of illegal substances, never steal or misuse company property, and never engage in behavior that could be construed as sexual harassment. So leave the contraband at home, never put un-earned company money or property in your pocket (more on this subject below), and eliminate sexual innuendo in your conversations with co-workers.

6. **Never be the instigator of rumor or gossip.** Some years back, the water cooler became a metaphor for an impromptu meeting area on company property. It might be the parking lot, the break room, the bathroom, or yes, even the water cooler. Regardless of where it takes place, it's the main distribution point for drama and distraction, with the topic usually centered

on office rumors. My advice? Stay out of it. Make it a point to protect yourself from the busy-bodies and blabbermouths who love to spread rumor, conjecture, and gossip. Management is always on the lookout for "agitators" who incite discontent or raise the anxiety level of other employees. If you're pressed for a comment, just smile and say nothing. Your response will leave the impression that regardless of whether you know or don't know, you're not saying anything about it. You're making it clear it's information you cannot or will not share—because you know better. Over time, you'll be respected for it. Yes, others may try to coerce or bait you into revealing what you know, and while the temptation to take the spotlight can be overwhelming, the rewards of keeping your mouth shut are far more valuable in the long run.

7. **Treat company email and inter-office correspondence as if it were public.** Here's an axiom for using email you should commit to memory: *Never put anything in your email correspondence that you wouldn't want to be said publically.* Email isn't secure, and after it's received, you no longer have any control over its distribution and who ultimately sees it. The same is true with any communication taking place under the company umbrella. Regardless of the assurance you've received confirming your conversation is private or privileged, once your words are part of a retrievable file, you've lost the advantage of plausible deniability. Worse, your comments and opinions—especially those containing innuendo or framed within a negative context—can be used against you if you're ever targeted to be managed out.

Use the company channels of correspondence for business only. Always use professional dialogue and avoid any personal references, slang, or innuendo. If you feel the need to criticize or convey an attitude, feeling, or suggestion that contains a negative inference about company policy, programs, customers, or employees, ask yourself what the repercussions would be if your email was broadcast to every employee within the company. In short, don't do it.

8. **Avoid revealing proprietary information in front of the competition.** It happens more frequently than you realize. You'll typically run into competitors at trade shows, marketing conventions, a customer's place of business, or industry association meetings. There's also the inevitability of seeing them in restaurants and other public places.

How do you behave when finding yourself face-to-face with a competitor? Here's a general rule: Be cordial and professional, and when it comes to business, *keep your mouth shut.*

Never, never, never (that's three in a row, so pay attention) talk about price, profit, markups, costs, market share, or anything having to do with money, customers, or a particular job or project. If you're overheard by someone who wishes to harm you professionally, you could be accused of collusion or price setting, a violation of anti-trust law.

When engaging the competition, smile, talk about the weather, the traffic, your trip to Yosemite, but steer clear of business. If the other person asks a question about your sales, a company project, or internal changes in responsibility or leadership, say you're not privy to that kind of information. Or, you can be more direct and respond with: "I can't say. As you know, those subjects are proprietary." Avoid phrases like, "I haven't heard," or "I suppose we'll find out later." This infers there is a situation under consideration, and that fact alone could be the very thing your competition wants to know. Asking about rumors, conjecture, and industry scuttlebutt is part of a competitive strategy—and it's your job to protect the company's secrets.

9. **Never steal from the company**. That includes using proprietary information for personal gain, accepting kickbacks

or bribes, manipulating a competitive situation to the financial advantage of one customer over another, or participating in any activity that diverts company money or assets into your pocket. As an employee, part of your job is to conserve and protect company property. And while I'm sure most recognize the illegality of stealing office furniture or computers, I'm referring to the more subtle but intentional manipulation of reports, records, or accounts that directly or indirectly results in personal financial benefit.

I can hear the groans now . . . "Hey, I *gotta* fudge a few bucks on the expense account to cover the miscellaneous charges. Otherwise, I'll never break even."

And I'm telling you, don't do it. Keep records of your reimbursable expenses as if your job depended on it. If you can't produce a receipt, don't submit it for repayment. Expense accounts have been used for decades to pad incomes, put gas into the spouse's car, and take the family out for a nice dinner. Moreover, those who do it think they're getting away with it.

The truth?

The accounting department, fleet managers, and Human Resources KNOWS. They talk about it over lunch—who's doing it, and how much was embezzled from the company this month. Think the term *"embezzled"* too harsh? Read on.

Dipping your hand into the corporate till—regardless of the amount—will hurt you in the long run. Your actions define your reputation. And if you can't be trusted to handle a couple of hundred dollars in an honest and forthright way, why would management put you in charge of thousands?

The same goes for local office managers who buy copy machines and desk computers for the office staff. If given local purchasing authority, make sure you collect evidence of having price shopped, negotiated for extra warranty periods, and obtained the very best price, terms, and conditions of sale *before you purchase.* Make it a habit to get everything in writing and save every quote and estimate. You never know when this can be useful to rationalize your choice of brand and vendor. Having to justify your choice may have nothing to do with an attack on your honesty, but could come in the form of a random audit. So be prepared to prove your best intentions by having a backup file of paperwork.

And while we're on the subject, let's talk about bribes, kickbacks, and slush funds. Beginning to feel uncomfortable? It's a common reaction, and that's because the flow of money *under the table* is a common problem in large companies. Product managers, sales associates, and marketing heads are continually being asked to cut prices to meet a competitive situation where none exists. In exchange, they're promised cash, or a cash-equivalent kickback (a bribe, if we call it what it really is).

For example, Distributor A asks their factory rep to give them a better price than Distributor B, their competitor. When Distributor A gets the business, the rep receives a "thank you" in the form of an expense-paid weekend to Vegas.

Kickbacks, slush money, and bribes can also originate from un-billed (free) replacement stock meant to replace "faulty" merchandise that never existed. It can also take the form of a "pass-through" discount (employee discounts, merchandise ordered as samples, or unjustified wholesale pricing) in which real value is exchanged, and one or more undeserving individuals receive a financial advantage. It's wrong and usually illegal.

Here's an objective way to determine whether an activity is questionable. Put yourself in the position of having purchased the company you work for. That's right; you own the whole thing, every desk, chair, and computer. The trash cans, staplers, and copy machines belong to you. You also pay everyone's salary. You own the company cars and pay for the gas to keep them running. Every month, you pay out tens of thousands of dollars for the building lease, utilities, and taxes. And when your company sells a product or service, you take a commensurate and reasonable amount for compensation, but most of the profit is used to pay for the continuing operation of the company.

Now, how do you feel about an employee who makes illicit arrangements to redirect money from your company's pocket into his? Still think it's a gray area?

Here's the acid test: If company management wouldn't approve of it, or you couldn't openly talk about it in front of the CEO, you've crossed the line.

The days of looking the other way are gone. The excuse of "Hell, everybody does it," won't fly. Here are three facts of life for employees who embezzle funds from their employer: (1) you *will* be found out. (2) You *will* lose your job. (3) You *may* go to jail.

Oh, and by the way, your reputation? It's in the sewer. Even if you're able to negotiate your way out of criminal charges, you'll have a blotch on your personal work history. If your misdeeds or financial impropriety results in a discharge for "nebulous" reasons—occasionally offered in exchange for a resignation—the resulting rumors will pretty much guarantee you'll never work in the industry again. People talk. And what was nebulous to some will be explained in great detail to others.

Look at it this way: Protecting the assets of your employer is protecting your livelihood. The company provides you with the financial resources to maintain your standard of living and invest in your future. Never endanger that relationship by taking advantage of your employer's trust—you'll only wind up stealing from yourself.

10. **Never openly or publically disagree with a supervisor or any member of a management team**. If you believe it is in the best interest of the company for an individual to be made aware of your opposing opinion (because you know something they don't), then objectively and privately present the new or overlooked information that substantiates your viewpoint. Make it clear your objective is for them to have all the facts before making a final decision, and regardless of what they decide, you will support it.

11. **Avoid making a legal claim (of any kind) against the company.** Regardless of your rights as defined by law, bringing formal legal action against your employer is applying the kiss of death to your career.

Granted, there are situations in which you may have good reason to go after the organization, but here's the real question: Do you plan to continue working there? If the issue can be resolved "off the books," you may be able to preserve your future with the company—*if you really want to stay*. However, if you take your grievances public with a formal complaint or lawsuit, you'll be labeled a whistleblower—a headache for the company and not someone they will want to keep.

The exception? If your complaint is clearly a case of discrimination or sexual harassment and after repeatedly and unsuccessfully trying to resolve the issue, you've reached the point where you've had enough. If this describes your situation, you need to take action to protect yourself. Check out the additional information in chapter nineteen. Hopefully, the suggestions you'll find there will provide you with a few defensive tools you can use.

12. **Keep the controversial and idiosyncratic parts of your life confidential**. I want to point out a few additional activities that might not seem to be a career risk, but can definitely slow or stall your advancement within the company. In extreme

cases—based on bias or the "moral compass" of management—engaging in any of the following activities can put you on the shortlist for termination. Luckily, any negative repercussions that might result from these "career killers" can be prevented by one simple action: *Keep the controversial and idiosyncratic parts of your life to yourself!*

For example, you may believe that using your backyard pool au-natural is a harmless, benign activity.

However, before you mention it during the morning coffee break, think again—your boss may find it offensive and even deviant. If it's not something you can read about in a family-friendly magazine, keep it to yourself. And that includes trips to provocative locations, resorts, or events.

Don't know what I'm talking about? In plain English, if you want to avoid being pigeon-holed as depraved or corrupt, stay away from the Hookers Ball in San Francisco, the adult entertainment award shows in Las Vegas, Fantasy Fest in Key West, or any other event that suggests or promotes "alternative" social or sexual behavior.

Regardless of the so-called "newly enlightened" attitudes that supposedly inhabit the upper floors of corporate America, we are still a country of conservative traditionalists. If you make it a point to broadcast or otherwise advertise your unconventional behavior, you may find yourself encountering all kinds of roadblocks unrelated to your work performance and productivity.

(Note: I'm not talking about an individual's primary sexual orientation. If you're gay or identify with a non-mainstream orientation, many states now have legal covenants in place to protect your lifestyle. Your choice of orientation or the gender of your life-partner should not impact your career path. If you believe it has, seek legal counsel.)

13. **Keep your investments and other income sources private.** Maybe you do a little consulting work on the side or edit manuscripts on the weekends, or manage social media for an online company. Although these activities are non-competitive and you perform them after regular work hours, they must remain a secret.

Your employer will, by default, consider other income-producing activities as threatening competition to your company career. In the myopic vision of management, an employee's attention and dedication to their job is diluted when they engage in other money-making activities, even when performed outside of regular working hours. Corporations are jealous masters, and they will not knowingly share their employees' commitment with other financially oriented activities.

In management's opinion, your off-hours should be spent recharging your batteries, so you return to work refreshed, ready to perform at peak efficiency. If your supervisor learns of your involvement in a sideline business or part-time venture, she'll blame any indication of stress, overwork, or distraction during working hours as a result of your outside activities, even though your symptoms may be the direct result of your day job.

14. **Never reveal serious personal health problems**. Except for a rare case of the sniffles, you should always project the image of someone who is in perfect health. Smoking, obesity, and excessive drinking are liabilities, and we've already discussed how companies feel about liabilities. In theory, your medical records are private, but a continuing chain of medical claims processed through the company insurance plan may prompt questions about your ability to perform your job. If taking time off for a doctor's visit or medical tests raises suspicions about your health, downplay the symptoms, and refer to any tests as "just routine."

15. **Use prudence and caution when posting on social media**. This includes Facebook, Twitter, Instagram, and all their various permutations. If you post something business-related, make sure it's positive and praiseworthy. Use extreme discretion if you post something personal. If it isn't something your mother, minister, or boss could read without you needing to offer an apology, don't do it. Anything suggestive, off-color, or having a sexual connotation is definitely off-limits. Plenty of employees have lost their jobs because they posted an inappropriate comment, revealed too much skin, or disclosed information that cast their employer in a negative light.

16. **Never discuss or disclose personal issues with anyone who could influence your career, either now or in the future**. Maybe you're having marital problems, or you're upset over the recent loss of a relative or pet, or you're just not feeling up to par. It happens. And it's human nature to take others into our confidence. But you're better off professionally if you keep your feelings to yourself. Revealing these issues—especially the details and how it's affecting you—can create doubt in the minds of those who are constantly evaluating your capability and competence. If management knows you're distracted or otherwise preoccupied with problems outside of work, they will assume you're off your game—your judgment is impaired and your priorities are in the wrong place. Revealing your personal plight may evoke all kinds of sympathy, but as far as management is concerned, you've just admitted you're not as effective as you could be, and if your disclosure takes place at the same time you're being considered for a promotion, you've just shot yourself in the foot.

What if you're blindsided? What if there are no warnings and you end up the target of an orchestrated effort to terminate you? As I said before, even the best employee can find themselves on HR's shortlist. The reason can be anything from an innocent mistake that angered a member of senior management, to a buy-out by a larger company, resulting in the elimination of your position or job function.

When HR strikes, you may be tempted to fight back. But never forget: *HR always wins.*

Right or wrong, they will prevail. Yes, we read about the occasional (pronounced *rare*) instance of an employee who stands up against unfair termination due to discrimination, legal infractions, or some other blatant disregard for personal rights. However, the vast majority of whistleblowers, martyrs, and champions-for-change pay an enormous price, both personally and professionally. And while I'll be the first to admit that the sacrifices made by some have been instrumental in improving the work environment for all of us, this book is written for the 99.9 percent of employees who want to use the corporate structure to not only survive, but to build a prosperous and satisfying life.

Having said that, I'll offer this to the 00.1 percent who've taken all they can take and are ready to fight back. I've provided a few suggestions in Chapter 20 titled, "Signs it's Time to Leave." Look under the subheading, "What if you're being harassed out?" It contains three specific actions you can use to defend yourself and lend credibility to your side of the story if you decide to pursue legal action.

Chapter Ten
Go With the Flow and Don't Rock the Boat!

Innovation and creativity are two of the most popular concepts in today's world of business. Often hailed as the twin keys to navigating change and meeting the challenges of a constantly evolving market, these "visionary" concepts have become the new cornerstones of success.

Sounds good, right?

Yes, innovation and creativity *sound* great! However, implementation—taking action to effect significant change within the corporation—can be the equivalent of playing Russian roulette with your career.

Why the contradiction?

Listen closely: Being the instigator of change puts the eyes of management squarely on *you*. Moreover, some of those eyes will belong to people who have a vested interest in leaving things exactly the way they are. Although they may respond with a head nod, or scribble the word, *interesting* on the bottom of your presentation or memo, they typically do not want you changing or being creative with what may have taken them years to put into place.

Granted, there are activities in your day-to-day work where you'll be given some flexibility or have the opportunity to do some independent thinking, but for the most part, large companies run on conformity—to the system, the policy, and to the standards used to determine satisfactory performance.

Stay focused on *your* job responsibilities and stay out of other people's business. In plain language, keep your nose where it belongs—pointed directly at your *assigned* responsibilities. You might think that suggesting a new method or system that saves money or improves effectiveness would be well-received. You might also think it would generate a lot of gold stars when it's time for evaluations and promotions. But that's not always the case. Initiating any kind of change comes with risk. Moreover, that risk and the possible negative impact on your career grow exponentially with the degree of change you're proposing. In short, the bigger the change, the greater the risk. Think of it in terms of escalating levels of career jeopardy: Small change equals small risk. Medium change equals a large risk. And big change equals an unacceptable risk. As a general rule, the degree of resistance you receive to your idea or suggestion will be directly proportional to the amount of change required to implement it.

For example, trying to improve or change a core system or process that has been in place for years can make you an especially vulnerable target. So before you become glassy-eyed with ambition and start suggesting modifications that are a radical departure from the way your company currently does business, stop and look at your actual work situation. Are your suggestions based on an objective assessment and a need to strengthen the company's position in the market? Or are you trying to bring attention to yourself as the brightest and most innovative guy or gal in the company?

Suggested changes and exceptions to the existing system should never be about YOU. This should be obvious, but I've seen lots of new hires who think of themselves as the entitled elite, deserving of special treatment. Unfortunately, this often includes the belief that the rules don't apply to them, and if necessary, the company should make an exception to established policies and practices to satisfy their personal wants and needs.

I'll illustrate the point with a brief personal story:

Three months after I was hired by Acme, I received a note from fleet management informing me it was time to order my first company car. My reaction? I was excited. Since the car would be mine to use, both on and off the job, it was a company perk I'd been looking forward to.

But my excitement didn't last long. After looking over the order form, I was disappointed in the choice of make and model. All the major brands were there, but I was limited to a full-size, four-door sedan with standard options, including cloth seats, non-premium colors, and basic wheel covers—a car my father would drive.

I wanted something sporty, the kind of vehicle that wouldn't require an apology when picking up a date (*Sorry about the ride, it's a company car*). I wanted a car that wouldn't embarrass me when pulling up in front of a friend's house, knowing their garage held a Mustang, or a Camaro, or (gulp) a Corvette.

I placed a call to the fleet manager and complained. "Don't you have other models I can choose from?"

"Those are the standard choices offered to all sales engineers," he said. "There are no exceptions."

He told me I was welcome to add options at my expense, but the choice of manufacture and model were not negotiable. They represented the image the company wanted to convey—conservative, reliable, dependable. The fact that I wanted a vehicle more characteristic of a car driven by a twenty-three-year-old single male was irrelevant.

"But I'm going to be spending a lot of time driving," I argued, "probably a couple of hours a day, and I would think the company would want that time to be as pleasant for me as possible. Doesn't management want me to be happy with the car?"

The fleet manager was silent for a moment and then said, "Remember, you're receiving a free vehicle. We pay all the operating expenses. Your financial responsibility is limited to the fuel used for personal mileage. You don't have to worry about the cost of insurance, registration, maintenance, or repairs, and we don't put any restrictions on personal use. You can use it on vacations and drive it anywhere in the United States. It's really a hell of a deal."

I tried again. "I understand the program. In fact, I calculated its value in dollars and cents when evaluating the company's job offer. I just didn't realize my choice of vehicles would be so limited."

The fleet manager took a deep breath. "The cars we offer our engineers are selected to convey the appropriate image to our customers," he said. "They provide excellent mechanical performance, and with normal maintenance, should . . ."

"But what if I'm out-producing my quota?" I interrupted. "I mean, if I'm bringing in an outstanding level of business, you'd probably make an exception and allow me to order something different, right?"

"I know you're new, so I'm assuming you haven't heard the story about Tony's car," the fleet manager said. Admitting I hadn't, he continued. "Tony worked out of the Denver office. He was a young guy and wanted to order a car that was "off-list." He knew the choices available to regional managers was broader and included several sports models. He decided if the company car program provided regional managers with more choices, it should do the same for a salesman working at 200% of quota."

"Two hundred percent? That sounds reasonable," I said. "He's making the company a lot of money. Recognizing his performance with a nicer car seems only fair."

"Our fleet program is not about being fair," the manager said. "It's about providing our people with the tools they need to get the job done."

"So what happened?" I asked. "Did he get the car he wanted?"

"No. And since he refused to make a choice from the standard models, we ordered a car for him, a mid-line Chevy in white, thinking that would be the end of it. But Tony was determined to make his point. After delivery, he had the right side of the car painted black, visually dividing the car in half. After the paint job, he added some paste-on flame decals on the doors and removed the wheel covers, but only on the black side. Depending on which side you were looking at, you got an entirely different impression. Tony said he would drive the company car, but he wanted everyone to know how unfairly he was being treated."

I wasn't sure what the fleet manager wanted me to say, so I asked, "How long did he drive the car that way?"

"Just the first day. As soon as his manager saw it, he told Tony to repaint the car at his expense. Tony took it as an ultimatum."

"That must have cost Tony a lot of money," I said.

"Yes, restoring the paint would have cost him a couple weeks' salary, but his final decision cost him a lot more than that."

"How so?" I asked.

"That was Tony's last day. The car sat in the parking lot for a few days, until we could get a local dealer to buy it. They repainted it and put it back on the lot."

"Sounds like nobody won," I said. "Tony lost his job, and the company lost a good salesman."

"You're half right," he said. "There's no argument that Tony lost his job."

Our conversation ended with me ordering a Ford Gran Torino with a few personally paid upgrades. It drove like a boat. Parking was a pain in the ass. To fully open the doors required finding a space without cars on either side. I hated it. But I drove it—until I was making enough money to buy the car I wanted.

My point in relating this story is to illustrate the importance of conforming to the system—especially when there's nothing to gain but your personal satisfaction. In Tony's case, he thought his performance warranted special recognition in the form of a company concession, effectively giving him the same privilege and status afforded to a regional manager. He either forgot or refused to acknowledge that his annual bonus was designed to serve that purpose, and the company car program was never intended to reward salespeople for doing a great job.

Tony also didn't consider the impression a more conservative car made on his customers, especially those over twice his age. Many of his customers no doubt considered the type of automobile he drove as an indication of his maturity and reliability—even if it was only a subconscious influence.

What about suggesting subtle changes, especially those you're sure will benefit the company? Before you can answer this question, you'll need to break down your work activities into two broad areas: (1) Your internal responsibilities and assignments, and (2) your external activities; what you do and say to those outside the company—your customers, vendors, and influencers.

Internally, it's steady as she goes. Don't even think of suggesting a change to the company's methods or procedures until you've been at your job for at least two years. Granted, that's taking a conservative posture, but it's also a safe one. Yes, a two year period of "internship" is a generalization, but it's a place to start when making an objective evaluation of your influence and perceived credibility. When you've been there long enough to be intimately familiar with the current administrative systems, then you can suggest *small* changes to existing practices, and only when you can demonstrate that it will save time or improve effectiveness.

"But wait, you argue, "what if making a large change will save the company a ton of money?"

I hear the rationale. But there are reasons some things are done in a specific—*and more costly*—way. And those reasons are often based on something other than money.

For example, let's say you discover a manufacturing or paperwork process that appears redundant. Seeing it repeated without obvious reason or rationale, you *believe* it's an obvious waste of money. But what if the redundancy you consider wasteful is necessary due to legal requirements, quality control, or some other aspect of the big picture you're not aware of? Or what if the duplicated effort *really is a waste*, and by eliminating it, the employee responsible for maintaining the system would be shown to be a gold-bricking, ineffective piece of deadwood?

And that person turns out to be the CEO's nephew?

At best, you'll be accused of "shallow thinking." You'll be criticized for not doing enough research, implying you weren't completely familiar with the system you wanted to change—a definite indication you're not ready to manage bigger and better things.

Always remember to count the cost of changing anything by determining *who* will be affected. Your suggestion to eliminate a time-wasting, non-productive or economically ineffective function may be spot-on. But if it results in a dozen people losing their jobs, it's probably not a suggestion that should come from you.

If you must be an agent of change, *adjust* **instead of transform.** Substitute, alter, and vary instead of revolutionize. Although you may not overwhelm others with your ingenuity and creativity (and then again, you might!), your efforts will demonstrate your concern about the company's effectiveness, and you'll poke fewer bears.

To give you an idea of how a simple suggestion to save time and increase effectiveness can backfire, here's a personal example that tested my relationship with my boss:

At Acme Corp, I was required to complete a weekly sales report. Details included whom I met with and a breakdown of the amount of time spent on each product when the presentation covered more than one. This data was used to determine how salespeople were spending their time relative to their assigned product quotas as well as forming the basis for charging the cost of sales burden to a particular product group.

Completing these forms was time-consuming. I spent an average of three hours a week filling them out, keeping them organized, compiling the data, and if necessary, modifying my product presentations (at least on the report) to ensure my face-to-face efforts would ultimately reflect my assigned sales goals.

After doing this for a couple of years, I realized I could save a lot of time by reverse-engineering my schedule to match my product quota. This meant using my quota assignment as a benchmark for matching specific products to the customers most likely to buy them, and then allocating my face-to-face time accordingly. Using a spreadsheet, I entered each of my customers into a database and assigned each one a priority based on its percentage of my total sales volume as a historical average. I added two additional metrics: the type and dollar value of product purchases to date, and what percentage of my total assigned quota in that product group those sales represented. After entering my sales activity for the week, I printed an update indicating where I needed to spend my time the following week—not only by product group, but also identifying which customer(s) I needed to see.

Now I had a system that provided weekly feedback on how I was spending my time. If necessary, I could make adjustments to keep my efforts in sync with my product responsibly. The real benefit was the time it saved. At the end of the week, I would enter the new data, punch a few keys, hit print, and that week's sales report was done. Not counting the several hours it took to set up the program, I reduced the time I spent generating the weekly sales report from three hours to about twenty minutes.

My first thought? Show it to my boss! I was sure he would shower me with accolades, congratulating me on creating a new time-saving process. I even envisioned him picking up the phone and calling the VP of sales, recommending me for raise—or dare I say it . . . a promotion!

His reaction?

"Don't show this to anyone," he warned me. "Yes, it automates the process, but you've included factors that provide for *corrective manipulation,* making the annual results a foregone conclusion."

"That's not the intent," I argued, "This provides immediate feedback on the difference between assigned product quotas and how a salesperson is *actually* spending their time. More importantly, the weekly cumulative totals indicate which products are in the most demand, so we can factor the dollar value of those sales against the time spent to generate it. Using this information, product managers can match their quota requirements to markets that demonstrate the greatest current need and make adjustments on a monthly basis. There's no need to wait for an annual review."

He shook his head. "The marketing department won't buy it. You're advocating that product sales should be driven by market demand, but our sales time is prioritized and allocated to the products that have received the most invested capital."

"Doesn't that sound backward to you?" I asked.

He took the usual deep breath I'd come to expect whenever we had one of our "heart-to-hearts."

The next half-hour was spent in one of the most stupid conversations I'd ever had with a manager. I should have let the subject drop, but I persisted. Eventually, he relented, permitting me to use the spreadsheet for my own reports, but only on the condition I never reveal it to anyone, including the other salespeople or office staff.

A week later, he confided that he recognized the value of my system, but he also knew the majority of the current product managers were too closed-minded and personally biased by personal agendas to recognize its value.

His cloaked compliment didn't help. From my perspective, I thought I was making a real contribution. But in reality, I was dabbling in areas outside my immediate assignment. The data resulting from my spreadsheet was the marketing department's responsibility to generate. Every year, they spent countless hours laboring over a formula to assign product quotas based on the profit they needed to rationalize a healthy return on investment, even when trade market reports indicated there was little or no actual market for the product. Suggesting they consider changing their approach—especially when the suggestion came from a member of the sales force—would be sacrilege!

The takeaway? Stay on your home turf. Trying to extend your influence into areas beyond your job scope can generate resentment and quiet anger. Worse, your well-intentioned recommendations may be interpreted as accusations that someone isn't doing their job—otherwise, why haven't they made the same suggestion?

You may have excellent ideas on how to improve some aspect of company operations, but if it's outside your "jurisdiction," you're going to be seen as meddling in places where you don't belong. As you move up in position and authority, you'll have plenty of opportunities to review company methods and processes, *when it falls under your job responsibility.* Avoid the fallout and possible career suicide by keeping your proposals for improvement focused on areas assigned to you.

Here's a relatively "safe" way of determining which systems and procedures can be changed or improved. Yes, there are changes that can be safely suggested, especially if they're likely to benefit the company in its *external relationships.* You'll typically have more latitude to improve situations, systems, and procedures outside the company than inside—as long as you don't create negative feedback or lose business.

Here's a simple example that worked: At Acme, one of my responsibilities was to call on architects and engineers who specified air conditioning chillers and air handlers as part of their design for large buildings and industrial plants. Many of these architects specified AC chiller equipment to be manufactured by the Trane Company. Trane had been an Acme customer for years, buying Acme electrical components for Trane's control consoles and electrical systems. But there was a catch: All of Trane's orders originated from a single location—the Trane corporate office in Wisconsin. This meant very little sales credit (about 15%) was given to field personnel located in the areas where the equipment was ultimately shipped and installed. This was a sore spot for a lot of us since any sales engineer with industrial control responsibility was expected to provide coordination and field service when Trane shipped equipment with Acme controls into their area. We could easily spend several hours to several days on a job site to correct a problem or when Trane supervisors requested a factory rep on-site to oversee some part of the installation and testing.

There was, however, a method by which a field rep could boost their sales credit. By notifying the Acme sales engineer in Wisconsin of Trane's impending order prior to its placement, the Acme field rep could increase their portion of the credit to fifty percent.

Realistically, the only way to do this was to stay in constant contact with the local Trane salespeople, hoping to learn of new and pending orders. In effect, the Acme rep had to stay ahead of Trane's internal order processing—a difficult challenge unless the rep literally made a nuisance of themselves by checking with the local Trane salesperson a couple of times a week.

With other customers' constant demand for our time and attention, being a "nuisance" was neither practical nor economically feasible. The result? With the amount of sales credit being so disproportionate to the amount of time required to service the account properly, many reps dedicated their priority to Trane on an "as needed" basis, hoping the need was minimal.

After a couple of years of being on the receiving end of this lopsided sales credit program (and spending way more time resolving Trane problems than I was compensated for), I decided to change the way I was communicating with the local salespeople at Trane.

On my next sales call, I dropped off a stack of pre-printed postcards. On the back, I included blanks for Trane's internal order number, job name, location, and needed delivery schedule. The front was addressed to me.

I explained that by having advance notice of upcoming projects, I could do a better job in communicating with our

Wisconsin office, and in some cases, improve delivery times for Acme's part of the job since we could allocate time in the manufacturing schedule before the order was officially entered into the system.

The Trane guys thought it was a great idea. Much of Acme's control equipment was custom built, and typical delivery time could stretch from three to six months. Being able to shave a few weeks off the production schedule would help ensure on-time delivery of the completed system to the job site.

Now here's the interesting part. This was nothing more than a simple stack of postcards, delivered with an explanation that emphasized the benefit to the customer. Personally, my motivation was based on receiving additional sales credit for fieldwork I was already doing. But the customer saw it differently. The local Trane manager wrote a letter to Acme headquarters commending me for my innovation and for recognizing that on-time delivery was a major challenge in supplying equipment to the final customer. More importantly, I'd done something about it.

Several weeks later, I was on a plane to Denver to make a presentation to all the salespeople in my region. The subject? How to use a pre-addressed postcard to expedite order processing, execute changes during construction, improve on-time delivery, and enhance communication between Acme and its customers.

Here's the takeaway: This type of change represented a low risk of repercussions in the event my idea was rejected by Trane. More important, it did not require any alteration to Acme's internal operation or processes.

Even so, the day following my Denver presentation, my manager confided that the Wisconsin salesman responsible for Trane's business had already complained about my postcards. Although they would allow him to provide an enhanced level of service to Trane, he would now have to give up an additional thirty-five percent of the sales credit he'd previously enjoyed. Thankfully, his complaints were ignored in deference to the compliments received from Trane, a significant and influential corporate account.

Here are three suggestions to help mitigate the risk associated with changing existing protocol, methods, or systems:

1. **Determine if your suggestion will affect your company's internal systems.** Hint: Modifications to *external* systems usually don't require company approval before implementing them. If you have even the slightest concern that your idea could affect any aspect of internal operations, you need to do a full stop until you can do an intensive risk assessment and discuss the idea with your manager. Let her opinion prevail.

2. **Do your best to extrapolate the worst-case scenario if your test fails**. How would failure affect your customers, vendors, or external influencers? Do you have a procedure for damage-control that will insulate all parties from liability or lost business? Here's the bottom line criterion for making the final decision: If there's a chance your suggestion could disrupt a customer's internal operations or result in negative feedback about you, your plan carries too much risk. Scrap it.

3. **If you're going to involve a customer, make sure you have excellent rapport with the customer's management and/or the owners.** Discuss the suggestion with them personally. Obtain their permission for a trial or test run of what you have in mind, with the promise of follow-up and evaluation before full implementation. Sell them on the advantages of your idea based on how it will benefit their operation in specific terms. For example, increased profits, employee engagement, cost savings, etc.

I'll wrap up this chapter with a final caveat. The idea of bucking the system because *we know we're right* is a fascinating concept. The notion of going our own way, of creating more independence and autonomy in our work—and being rewarded for it—is intoxicating, especially with the business media inundating us with stories about those who broke the rules and came out on top. It stirs us with that rebel-mindset we all harbor at some level.

But I'm telling you, don't take the risk. Expressing your inner maverick is a great marketing teaser to sell books and magazines. However, in the real world of eight to five, conducting yourself in unconventional ways, or taking action based on impulsive or spontaneous motives that are in contradiction to conventional and accepted methods—especially within the traditionally conservative environment of the corporation—will likely get you terminated.

Until you've sat in a manager's chair for a couple of years (regional level or higher), you'll be expected to adapt to the company's existing policies and procedures—not the other way around. Ask any long-term, successful corporate employee and the majority will strongly recommend accomplishing your career goals by using the existing company architecture and adhering to the established methodology—if you want to be recognized for your accomplishments and stay out of trouble.

Chapter Eleven
Bring the Right Kind of Attention to Yourself

Long-term career success is rarely dependent upon performance alone. Yes, doing a good job and getting results are important, but they are not the *most* important traits of those who enjoy the benefits of corporate success.

What makes the defining difference? There are three unbreakable rules for corporate longevity. For decades, they have been the cornerstones of a valued and highly compensated employee . . .

Rule One: Play by the rules. No, I'm not being facetious. I'm telling you that your talents, performance, and ultimate contribution will be more likely appreciated *and rewarded* when you stay between the lines, follow the standard protocol, and use the existing channels of communication and execution.

Those who take the time to learn and understand their company's systems and procedures—*and use them*—will receive recognition for a job well done. See some room for improvement? A little tweak here and there can bring congratulations and promotions. However, be careful! As we previously discussed, suggestions to scrap the status quo and make wholesale replacements can bring disapproval and criticism, especially when the procedures under scrutiny were originated by company patriarchs.

Rule Two: You must meet the expectations of your superiors. Keep in mind these may be different for each ascending level of management. Your regional manager may want to see you spending the majority of your time pursuing new customers and developing future business over the long term. The vice-president, however, may believe the future success of the company is dependent upon removing the deadwood. His goal may be to consolidate sales territories and reduce expenses. So while he will no doubt recognize an aggressive and determined approach, his evaluation of your efforts will more likely be focused on your capacity to assume additional responsibility and handle a heavier workload, without the loss of existing business.

The key is to satisfy the obvious needs of each manager without using "under the table" memos, different versions of the same report, or other "behind-the-back" communications. We'll get into the nuts and bolts of this process later.

Rule Three: How others perceive you is more important than what you accomplish. Most of your success in a corporate environment will depend not on what you actually do, but on what others *believe* you do, as well as what they think you can do in the future. Although their opinion may, to some extent, be based on the outcomes you've achieved in the past, their *perception* of your skills, talent, attitude, and loyalty is often as important as your bottom-line results.

Jeffrey Pfeffer, a professor at the Stanford Graduate School of Business, confirmed this idea with a study that showed those who made a good impression on their boss received better performance reviews than those who worked harder but were not as highly thought of.

Is that fair?

No, it's just the truth.

If you're going to work for the corporation—and receive all the benefits it offers—you need to understand how the real world of corporate business operates and use that knowledge to your advantage.

Rule Four: The key to long-term corporate survival is compromise. When working for any large company, an individual's longevity is typically a reflection of their ability to compromise. As an employee, you'll be asked to do things that seem silly, wasteful, unnecessary, or downright stupid. You may even be used as a scapegoat, expected to take the heat, and still respond with a professional, "Company-First" attitude. And make no mistake, while you're scrambling to keep the lid on your personal feelings, every move you make, every word you say, will be watched, listened to, and evaluated. How you respond under pressure often defines future opportunities, so keep the bigger picture in mind.

Here are a few of the typical questions a boss uses to appraise their subordinates:

Is this person a "company" man or woman? Is he or she worth keeping?

Should she be considered for promotion?

Is he the kind of person I want representing this company to customers?

Your job—your highest priority—is to make sure the answers reflect a constant stream of yes's. And that's true even if you don't plan on staying with the company in the long term.

Rule Five: Your ability to influence your assignment and career path is directly related to your knowledge of the company's current business activities, priorities, and future plans from a national (or international) perspective. You need to keep an eye on at least two market locations outside of the one in which you're currently working. In specific terms, this means being familiar with the general competitive activity, current and historical market share for the past three years, and any new development or demographic information that might impact the company's business in those locations.

Why become familiar with alien markets?

Being knowledgeable about the bigger picture is the fastest and most effective way to convince management to stop thinking of you as another company drone and consider you as an informed and invested employee—someone who deserves more respect than the guy who just shows up, puts in his time and goes home.

How does this manifest itself in personal power and influence? It can give you leverage when you need it the most.

For example, let's say a branch manager's job has opened up in Crapville, Arizona, where the summers are 130 degrees in the shade, and the Gila monsters are large enough to carry off your French Poodle. After being asked to consider the job, you politely explain that you believe your efforts would be better served in Denver or Tampa, because you've been reviewing the losses in market share in those locations and have some marketing ideas to turn the situation around, which coincidentally, would result in additional bottom line profits to the company.

Suddenly, the conversation is no longer about Crapville, Arizona.

"Tell me more about our decreasing market share in Denver," your boss says. "You sound like you've got a real handle on what's going on there."

In practical terms, staying up-to-date about your company's business means paying close attention to the current influences in the company's *national* marketplace, and at least two specific regions or trade areas within it.

How do you stay current on markets other than your own? At least once a week, search the internet for new articles and information. Use your company's name, products (if unique), and your company's three main competitors as search terms. This will provide you with plenty of information to slip into conversations when appropriate.

Yes, it's extra work, but it can be an effective defense against a sudden or unexpected offer of a transfer to an undesirable location.

The downside? You may have to make good on your alternative suggestions. In the example of being offered a move to Crapville, Arizona, it could mean exploring and even moving to the alternative location(s) you proposed. But in most cases, pursuing those alternatives—ones you've personally suggested—will be the lesser evil, and will provide you with a lot more control over your career in the long-term.

Chapter Twelve
Get Caught Doing the Right Thing

A large part of influencing your superiors is having them acknowledge you as someone who "does the right thing." But before we talk about the specific activities that can accelerate career advancement, there's an important pre-requisite that must be in place to ensure you get the maximum benefit from your effort.

You must make sure your boss knows what you're doing.

Assuming your supervisor will automatically notice your daily achievements is taking a huge risk. The boss is busy. And she can't constantly monitor your activities. *Catching employees doing something right* is an old management concept, but the necessary time investment makes it nearly impossible to implement consistently. This means it's up to you to bring your daily victories to the boss's attention.

What qualifies as a "victory?" Sometimes it results from concentrating your attention and actions on a specific problem. Other times it comes from a spontaneous reaction to a challenging situation. But with some creative interpretation, either situation can be explained as a series of logical, well-executed, response-based choices that reflect your skill, talent, and experience.

And that brings us back to the problem: When you're busy demonstrating all that clever expertise, where's your boss? There's a good chance she's out of the office, or in a meeting, or on the phone.

So how do you make sure she learns about your most recent success?

You're going to keep a record of your achievements, both great and small. Dedicate a notebook for this specific use, documenting who was involved, when and where it took place, and what happened. Include relevant details and use a consistent format. Keeping these records uniform and coherent will add credibility when presenting this information during an evaluation. This also helps to frame your "success diary" as an objective and professional record of your performance, instead of a grandstanding attempt to toot your own horn (more about this below).

As we review the five steps of creating an effective diary format, keep in mind the specifics of *your* achievement record will depend on your job responsibilities and daily activities, so don't hesitate to change something to fit your personal circumstances.

1. Start with a brief description of the problem, miscommunication, or situation that needed to be resolved. If there were two sides to the event, describe both.

2. Describe the options that were available and what you believed would be the expected result from each one.

3. Explain why you took the action you did, and the final result you achieved. Include any downstream effect on subordinates, customers, or others affected by the outcome.

4. In hindsight, confirm that you would or would not make the same decision now. Explain why, and if you believe your actions should have been different, include a brief description of what you learned and how you plan to implement it in the future.

5. Include any feedback obtained from co-workers, customers, vendors, or others who were involved in the situation.

When is the best time to present your accomplishments to your supervisor? There's no better time for a little self-promotion than during your annual or semi-annual review.

Never leave this formal review process to chance. It's one of the most important meetings you can have with your supervisor, and you should use this time to proactively substantiate your value to the company (translation: to keep your job) and to show your supervisor you've made significant progress in increasing your productivity.

How do you make your presentation without appearing pretentious or self-important? First, don't march into your boss's office, open your notebook, and start bragging about yourself. Explain that your notebook is a collection of "learning experiences." And you've been documenting situations and circumstances in which you exercised your current level of training and expertise with the intention of obtaining supervisory feedback to determine if your actions could have been improved.

See the difference? You've just characterized your notebook as a personal training and evaluation tool, creating the opportunity for your boss to comment on your work, and to make suggestions on how to improve your productivity in the future.

What about situations that are not "notebook worthy?" Your notebook is reserved for examples that demonstrate your knowledge, expertise, and communication skills—instances when you demonstrated your value to the company. Avoid diluting the impact of these events by jotting down every little action you take on behalf of others. Yes, these "small contributions" can be time-consuming and often go unrecognized due to the on-going activities of a busy day, but they don't belong in your notebook.

So how do you make sure the boss is aware of your recurring efforts to contribute to a more positive working environment? If you spent time on an internal situation, write a short note to the other employee(s), thanking them for their input and contribution. Make sure the content is positive and offers praise for their efforts. If your role was strictly assistive, let them know you're available for any follow-up questions or concerns. Copy your boss on all correspondence. Use the same process to acknowledge the efforts of a team leader, division supervisor, or other management head to acknowledge a contribution that directly affected your team, section, division, or customers. And always copy your boss when sending positive comments to a customer. (Note: Never put anything negative about a customer in writing, even if your comments are supposedly for internal use only.)

The second part of "doing the right thing" is to concentrate on the things that count. Some activities will count in your favor more than others, even though some of these actions will not necessarily be customer-centered or profit-driven. Very few *large* companies are truly focused on their customers as their first and only priority. (You may want to read that again.) Yes, management will typically claim they are, and will often put up a convincing argument with customer feedback programs, loyalty discounts, enhanced customer service, extended guarantees and return periods, technical service hotlines, and so on. But when these programs become too costly, or it's shown that profits can be increased by eliminating them, the priority typically shifts.

(The question of which comes first—customer satisfaction or profit—is analogous to the proverbial riddle about the chicken or the egg. Maximizing profit to the detriment of customer service is just as dangerous as over-serving the customer to the point that the resulting—and necessary—price increase becomes uncompetitive. Finding a reasonable balance between profit and service requires implementing less costly ways of providing *productive* levels of customer service while maintaining—or ideally, increasing—market share and consumer loyalty. In this case, "productive" means a measurable increase in business as a direct result of customer service. For example, if the termination of all customer service programs results in zero change to the company's business, you could conclude that the company's service program was ineffective, outdated, or unnecessary. It wasn't helping to generate more business, which is a strong indication that the program needs an overhaul and/or an upgrade—which *could* increase the business level.)

As a general rule, all company activities—including customer service—must eventually contribute to growing the profit of the organization. From the standpoint of maintaining the company's operations and continued growth, profit always sits in judgment over all other company functions.

I mention this because many employees believe the success of their career is primarily dependent on how well they serve their customers, either directly or through company programs designed to increase customer satisfaction. However, regardless of the latest company rhetoric about building and enhancing customer relationships, you should realize your *personal* success is ultimately determined internally—by management—and not by the company's customers, who incidentally, support the financial health of the company by buying its products and services.

Need proof? I've seen dozens of salespeople, customer service reps, and transaction coordinators build a devoted and appreciative following of customers, then lose their jobs during take-overs and reorganizations simply because they were not management's favored candidate. Always remember, corporate success is an inside job.

Activities That Raise Your Perceived Value in the Eyes of Management

Going "above and beyond" your assigned responsibilities is one of the best ways to boost your perceived value to management. And the good news is that you can do it without working an extra ten hours a week or giving up your Saturday golf game. Here are three examples of activities that typically raise management's opinion of your value in both the short and long term.

Participate in company training classes, seminars, and correspondence courses. Companies expect their employees to take advantage of training options on an on-going basis, not only for the learning experience but also as an indication of their commitment to their job. In effect, the company is offering an opportunity to increase your skills and knowledge. Responding with hesitancy or even co-operative neutrality is not what they want to see. They want an employee who responds with an eager desire to be a part of the company's future. From management's perspective, your *enthusiastic* participation is often more important than what you learn.

If the training is lengthy (for example, a two-day seminar), read the material ahead of time to be able to discuss it intelligently in class. Think of questions to ask and examples to use. This is not the time to avoid being the "teacher's pet." You're there to impress, and your behavior will be evaluated and reported to management.

Always take notes and jot down ideas on how to incorporate the training into your job responsibilities. Is the subject something you could modify or adapt (without copyright infringement) and present to your subordinates or customers? Being able to teach others in a formal setting is a valuable asset, and volunteering to do customer training will definitely get you noticed.

Don't skimp on the paperwork. We all hate paperwork. Unfortunately, corporations run on paper. Cut one open, and it bleeds charts, graphs, and spreadsheets. Leave the wound open for an hour, and the ground will be covered in memos, employee evaluations, policy directives, market share analysis, cost-benefit comparisons, customer surveys, and . . . the list goes on and on.

Is all that paper really necessary? It depends on whom you ask.

Marketing will emphasize the importance of their pie-charts. It's the only way to demonstrate an intangible asset, they'll say. (For example, the value of branding can be broken down into its components of customer loyalty, name and logo recognition, and peer-influence).

Salespeople want a clearly defined compensation plan, and they want it in writing (to avoid "misunderstandings" on payday).

The engineering department worships their technical drawings, descriptions, and testing data. (Ironically, they rebel at the sight of correspondence requiring them to rationalize expenditures, cost-overruns, and missed product deadlines.)

The real loser in the paperwork nightmare? The administrative assistant. They must process, collate, file, duplicate, and distribute all that paper.

For those of you trying to remind me of the advent of the "paperless office," I'll concede that the advantages of digital storage and retrieval have made a drastic reduction in the amount of physical paper that used to cover everyone's desk. But there are still plenty of companies that maintain a physical paper backup of strategic and irreplaceable documents. While some of these are intrinsically important, such as deeds, patents, and legal settlements, their paper storage may also contain more routine correspondence, such as employee exit interviews, customer contracts, and vendor agreements.

Here's a common policy when it comes to retaining physical paperwork: "If it carries an ink signature, it goes in the filing cabinet."

What does this mean to you? In larger, multi-divisional companies, the amount of paper you generate is often an indication of your productivity (or the lack of it). The key is to make *your* paperwork add to your presence in a positive way. Countless managers owe their career advancements to the fact that they dazzled the boss with paperwork. It may seem like a repetitive, simple-minded waste of time, but in the eyes of management, a continuous stream of detailed and well-composed paper demonstrates your enhanced communication skills—an indication of your ability to clearly translate your ideas and thoughts to others. That alone will take you a long way down the corporate road to career success.

View your personally-generated correspondence as not only written confirmation of your activities but also a validation of the importance of your work. It's a way to bring management into *your* loop—the one that eventually leads to a promotion.

Take every opportunity to use your public speaking skills. Let's start with a true story. The first time I was asked to speak in a business setting, I was caught unaware and unprepared—in front of an audience of about fifty people.

My boss had just introduced me as the new account rep for a large distributor chain. After reciting a brief synopsis of my background, he invited me to the front of the room to "say a few words."

As I rose slowly from my chair, I felt the blood leave my brain. I wondered which would be less damaging to my career . . . passing out on the way to the podium, or standing behind it with my face frozen, unable to speak, my hands shaking like twin jack-hammers.

What happened? In the fifteen seconds it took to walk to the front of the room, I put together a quick speech based on the fact that I *was* new, would need to learn more about the distributor's business operation and customer base, and I would ask the fifty people in the room to have patience with me. In return, I would promise to help solve their challenges with competitive pricing, technical presentations to their customers, and to always be available for joint sales calls, which would add credibility to their representation of our products.

My "speech" lasted less than two minutes. It was a little awkward, contained an un-necessary pause or two, but I got through it. I didn't pass out, throw up, or wet my pants. And when I returned to my seat, I had the most unexpected reaction.

I enjoyed it!

The following week, my boss asked me if I wanted to teach a series of training classes for two dozen new hires from a large distributor account. Before my forced introduction to public speaking, I would have made one excuse after another, hoping I could talk my way out of it. Instead, I accepted immediately.

I realize my experience may not be typical. But the point is, *I was scared*—at first. Then I took the first step and my brain kicked in, saving my ass. Here's the good news . . . You don't have to face your first public speaking experience unprepared. Preparation is the key, *because it will happen.* At the least likely time and place, your boss will turn to you and say, "Take over for me while I make a phone call. Just keep them occupied until I get back."

If that thought makes you break out in a cold sweat, don't worry. There are plenty of excellent professional speakers who experience the same level of apprehension every time they stand in front of an audience. Even after giving hundreds or even thousands of presentations, they still experience a case of butterflies before walking on stage. Hearing their name spoken during the introduction, they feel their pulse quicken, their stomach tighten—just like they did the very first time they made a presentation. But now, they not only expect that heightened level of anxiety; they welcome it. They depend on that surge of nervous energy to raise their level of performance and give their presentation a real shot in the caboose.

Still not sure about how public speaking could impact your career? Answering a request to make a simple comment or two will get you remembered as someone who rose to the occasion, didn't hesitate, and had the courage to take the lead. Conversely, turning down a speaking request will also leave an impression—as someone who had nothing to say when others were willing to give you their time and attention. You let them down, and you left them disappointed.

Never discount an opportunity to speak as unimportant. You can't anticipate who might be in the audience. Impressing a stranger with your presentation can lead to conversation, networking, and even new career opportunities. And as I've shared with my own example, it's a powerful way to gain recognition from your current employer.

If you want to know more about how to control your nerves and make a spontaneous speech or presentation, I suggest picking up a copy of *Speak Up! A Step-by-Step Method to Conquer Your Fears and Give an Amazing Speech* by yours truly.

Progressive techniques for *always* being seen doing the right thing.

The suggestions in this final section of the chapter are based on activating a "professional mindset." And while that may sound like clichéd rhetoric from a motivational poster, these specific activities, fortified with adjustments to your attitude, can help you create the impression of a focused professional, regardless of the day's activities.

1. **Be generous with your knowledge and skill**. If a co-worker asks for help, and you can accommodate their request without jeopardizing a deadline or high priority task, spend fifteen minutes with them. Longer periods of time should be scheduled and approved by your manager. As a general rule, you should make a point of offering help to a subordinate or team member who needs it. Determine their weaknesses and either help them to complete the work, or if within your responsibility, reassign the task to someone more experienced who can provide step-by-step instruction. Why go to all the extra effort? If a co-worker or subordinate's performance is substandard, your manager probably knows it, and your efforts to help them will not go unnoticed.

2. **Make decisions within a timeframe that makes you appear discerning, informed, and effective.** Use the data you have at hand. Based on the circumstances and situation, determine if waiting is likely to produce new information that will make a difference in your decision. Most important, estimate how long you can wait before NOT deciding will put you at a disadvantage. Finally, ask yourself if you are making a calculated decision or taking a gamble—one is defensible, the other is not.

3. **Stay in emotional control,** especially when the news is negative. Keeping a steady hand on the wheel is the mark of a leader, and as I've said before, someone is always watching.

4. **Maintain the balance of power in both directions**. Allow your manager to exercise her prerogative, influence, and authority. Accept her decision as final and support it. Never express a negative opinion about her or her ideas to anyone while she is employed by the same company. Conversely, never show weakness, indifference, or negativity in front of your subordinates. Treat them with respect and let them know you expect the same.

5. **Accept criticism without becoming defensive**. If a superior is stupid enough to criticize you in front of your team, never cower or grovel. Say something like, "I appreciate your thoughts, and I'll use them to prevent the problem from re-occurring in the future."

6. **Maintain your flexibility.** Your ideas for change or improvement may be practical, well-considered options, but no one will believe in them as strongly as you do. You are one voice among many, and even when you know your plan is superior to others under consideration—including the one ultimately chosen—you must adopt and support the company's final decisions as if they were your own. Your endorsement of company policies and methods will go a long way in motivating others to validate your opinion about future projects. You never want to be suspected of direct or indirect sabotage because you were opposed to a new company program or policy.

7. **Don't allow low-priority tasks to reduce your professional mindset**. A lot of your day-to-day actions will not always be about bringing in the new mega-account or solving a major problem that results in immediate praise and recognition. There's going to be a lot of time spent on routine functions. This can be anything from helping the office manager inventory the copy paper, resolving billing errors, or placating the habitually demanding customer by feeding him a Grand Slam at Denny's.

During these "maintenance" days, when you're consumed with seemingly low priority tasks, there's always the risk of reduced focus—of coasting through the process. You don't deliver at one hundred percent because there's no need. You can get the job done with your brain working at a slow idle. In fact, you can take care of everything while listening to your favorite music in one ear and perusing over vacation options on your laptop—or so you think.

"Coasting" through the workday is similar to an actor who walks on stage and looks out across an auditorium that's only ten percent occupied. Why should he bother to give the same level of presentation he gave last week when the house was packed?

Because it's who he is.

He doesn't compromise his performance just because there are fewer people to appreciate it. The people who did show up still expect to see his very best. If the actor slacks off or allows the lower level of audience energy to affect his delivery, he knows it will show. Just like he knows that even though the audience is small, if they're impressed, they'll tell others.

Adopting a professional attitude is part of being recognized as a leader—someone who is responsible, dedicated, and promotable—the very attributes you want to convey to those who can do the most for your career.

Chapter Thirteen
Meetings: They're Not Going Away,
So Make Them Serve You!

Like them or not, meetings are an integral part of the corporation. Spontaneous meetings have become an uncontrollable epidemic. Often prompted by little more than the desire to "get everyone together," managers use meetings as a tool to motivate and monitor their subordinates.

Whether it's implementing a new organizational process, a strategy session, dissecting a team report, setting goals, implementing policy changes, or disseminating information, a face-to-face meeting is still the preferred method to accomplish the task.

I know of several companies with a standing schedule of a one-hour meeting every Friday morning to discuss whatever topic may be on the minds of the employees. This is a meeting to discuss *anything* related to the business, with no planned agenda or subject.

The biggest challenge with any meeting is making it as productive as possible. And while lots of attention has been focused on a manager's responsibility to create a positive group dynamic, there are many ways in which you—as an attendee—can influence the tone and ultimate outcome of any meeting, even when you are not the presenter or speaker.

First, realize that as a meeting participant, your exposure, and the degree of your influence is inversely proportional to the number of participants in the room. In other words, if you're in a meeting with 500 other people, you tend to get lost in the crowd. However, if the boss calls you and ten of your co-workers together to brainstorm the latest marketing program, your impact on others—your overall impression—is typically being evaluated and judged by everyone in the room. In fact, the smaller the meeting, the more your behavior will impact your credibility—long after the meeting is over.

The following suggestions are based on techniques designed to help you impress and persuade, regardless of whether you're meeting one-on-one, or in a room with fifty people:

1. Match eye contact time with whoever is speaking—with an emphasis on the word "match." Maintaining constant eye contact can be just as bad as never looking directly at the speaker. Try to balance your "eyes on" and "eyes off" time with the occasional head nod.

2. Practice your smile. Make sure it appears authentic. Your smile makes a huge impact on others, especially when they're forming a first impression. It conveys the message that you're engaged and listening—and you like what you hear. It's a powerful feedback device, so use it to your advantage.

3. Remember everyone's name. If there's someone in the group you don't know, jot down their name at the beginning of the meeting. If you can't remember it or didn't hear it, ask them to repeat it immediately.

4. Before the official start of the meeting, don't hesitate to use "small talk." It allows communication to begin without the risk of exposing your ideas and opinions too soon. If you need to start the ball rolling, ask, "How's your day going, on a scale of one to ten?" Unless the answer is "ten" (it seldom is), say, "Let's see if we can't move that to a higher number." (I wish I could credit the originator of this exchange, but I have no idea who it is; I overheard it used by a seminar attendee and thought it was worth repeating.)

5. Have some idea of what you want others to take away from the meeting—*and from meeting you.* These are often not the same thing. Your goal is to leave others with a positive

impression after interacting with you—to ensure they continue to be receptive to future communication and business. Promote your agenda, but keep it flexible and don't push or force your ideas and opinions on others in an effort to make your point.

6. Test the timing. What's the mood of the decision-makers? How receptive are they to listening to others? Do they seem rushed, distracted, or preoccupied? Rather than risk an automatic "No" to your proposal or suggestion—because the decision-makers are overwhelmed with other business or personal matters—hold off on suggesting a new idea or making an important presentation until you have a more receptive audience.

7. Pace subtle aspects of body language exhibited by others in the room, *especially the one talking*. Mirroring others helps establish subliminal levels of rapport. This is an extremely powerful technique and can help increase your influence over others.

8. If you're meeting with customers, avoid over-the-top clothing or accessories that divert attention away from you and toward your possessions. People want to do business with those who make wise financial decisions. You might impress a few people with a $10,000 Rolex, but the majority of the wealthy and successful may question not only how you manage *your* money, but how you would manage *their* money as well.

9. Be in your seat five minutes early. If you don't want to appear overly anxious or you need to prevent any pre-meeting conversation that could lessen the leverage of your planned contribution, arrive early and wait in the car or restroom until you can walk through the door exactly on time.

10. Eliminate "up-talking." It's become an epidemic. Also called "up-speak," it's a vocal rise at the end of a declarative sentence. Studies show 70% of the population find it annoying and will judge you less intelligent or credible for doing it.

11. Adhere to the 80/20 rule: Listen 80 percent of the time, talk 20 percent. If there are more than three people in the meeting and everyone is taking turns speaking, reduce your speaking time accordingly unless you're asked for details, feedback, or to expand on the subject. If you need to create more *productive* speaking time in a larger group, first ask for someone's opinion about the subject. This typically provides you with the opportunity to thank them for their input, comment on their contribution, and segue to the point you want to make.

12. When replying to the last person speaking, match their rate of speech for the first two sentences, then move to your usual speed.

13. Avoid interrupting. Interruptions are unprofessional and impolite. Wait for a silent count of "two" before speaking.

14. Ask questions. "Do you have the details on that? What's the down-side (or up-side) of the situation? How did you handle that particular challenge?" To avoid overwhelming the speaker, ask one question at a time.

15. Never check your cell phone or answer a call during a meeting. Giving your cell phone priority over those in attendance is rude and demeaning. You agreed to meet for a reason. Don't make others regret their decision.

What if you don't have anything to say? If you have nothing to say (because you're unfamiliar with the subject or haven't had a chance to do any homework), it's going to be difficult, and maybe even risky, to make an intelligent comment. However, sitting quietly without offering any input or feedback also carries a risk, suggesting you're not interested, you're bored, or not a team player. If you find yourself in this situation, consider using one of these strategies:

1. Confirm you've reviewed the opposite viewpoint of the one being discussed. You don't present the opposing opinion or alternative as an argument, but as a helpful side comment. This implies you've looked at the situation from the alternative standpoint, and can't find the same advantages as the one favored by management. In other words, you're in agreement, and you're offering your personal validation that the boss has done a good job, effectively placing a halo on the head of your superior (*the halo effect*). In most cases, you won't need to reveal what the alternatives are, because you've confirmed that the best choice is the one currently on the table.

By the way, this can also give others the impression that you're a big-picture guy—someone who is creative and can generate useful ideas and viewpoints, even when you bring nothing new to the discussion.

2. Become the fly on the wall. Another way to generate useful comments during a meeting is to transition your perspective to "third-position." This means mentally lifting yourself above the conversation and viewing the interchange as if you were a fly on the wall. Ask yourself what's taking place between the participants? Is it positive, negative, or neutral? What's missing or needs to be said? What could you add to support management's position based on a specific experience or a previous situation?

3. Ask questions that can be answered with a positive response. This simple technique is surprisingly powerful and can help you make a great impression. The key is to ask questions in such a way that implies a supportive attitude. Here's an example:

Our company had adopted the concept of Management by Objective (MBO) as a motivational tool to use with wholesale distributors. Implementation of the program required hours of preparation and face-to-face planning with distributor management, as well as a rigorous schedule of on-going evaluation and documentation. It was, in a nutshell, a time-consuming, paperwork nightmare that promised to be a royal pain in the ass.

After our boss introduced the program, he asked for comments. One of the new hires asked the question that was on everyone's mind: "Isn't this just another bunch of forms that have to be filled out, creating more paperwork, and adding to the customer's perception of our company as being overly concerned with administrative oversight?"

The boss was silent for a moment and then agreed that it was certainly one possible reaction. Before he could continue, another new hire jumped in with this question:

"What if we use this as a planning tool to determine the resources the distributor needs to do a better job at selling our products? Any resistance we receive from management could be countered by offering additional training for their sales force with an offer to accompany them on sales calls. Having the factory rep along would give their salespeople greater credibility and open more doors. We could even sponsor a contest to reward their top salesperson with a plaque and a gift certificate to a nice restaurant."

The result? The guy who asked the first question left before the end of the year, complaining about the lack of advancement opportunities. The second guy—who, by the way, in my opinion, had the least likely set of skills to manage anyone—was promoted to a regional position within 18 months.

Did their respective career success with Acme have anything to do with integrating the MBO program into their customer network? No, not specifically. However, what did make a difference was their receptivity, support, and general attitude *as it was perceived by management.*

There are always questions you can generate about a new topic or subject. Just make sure your questions convey your support, while casting the subject and management in a positive light.

Advanced strategies for private, one-on-one meetings

One-on-one's are typically reserved for performance reviews, exchanges of proprietary information, or when the boss wants you to know you're being considered for possible advancement, a special assignment, or termination.

One of the worse things that can occur during a private meeting with your boss is to be asked a question you're not prepared to answer. Unexpected questions hitting you blindside not only opens the possibility of sticking your foot in your mouth, it can also make you appear uninformed and incapable of thinking on your feet.

Your best defense?

Ask for permission to set the question aside for a few minutes. This reduces the pressure to answer with an off-the-cuff comment that could easily disclose your ignorance about the subject. In many cases, it also diffuses the perception of being unprepared and gives you time to think of an acceptable answer. If your boss insists on a first impression or an immediate response, say "I've been researching the possible outcomes, and I really want to get this one right. I know how important it is to make sure we've covered all the contingencies, and I have just a few more sources to check. Can we revisit this in an hour or so?"

For example, you could ask for a few minutes to make a follow-up phone call that will provide that final piece of information you've been waiting for. Explain that it's the last piece of the puzzle you need to produce the most accurate answer possible. This implies you've been working on the subject and are close to bringing it to a conclusion. Then use the time to your best advantage.

If the question is in the form of an ultimatum . . . consider your list of non-negotiable items. These are your reasons—justifications—for why you work at ABC corporation in the first place. It's also why it's important to create your list of bottom-line, "must-have" needs upfront, and periodically review them as circumstances dictate.

If you have to give in on one or more of your priorities in the short term, but believe there's a good chance of coming out ahead in the long run, it's usually the better choice to give in and set a date (with yourself) to review your progress under the compromised conditions. If you go this route, avoid revealing any personal reservations or exhibiting any hint of negativity to your supervisor.

The flip side? If compromising one or more of your "non-negotiables" is going to affect your happiness, your relationship with your family, or your gut reaction is a strong "No," it's a red flag, and you should weigh the consequences very carefully. Remember, it's why you made your list of personal priorities in the first place.

If you feel the discussion is going against you . . . and a decision is about to be made that is not in your best interest, ask for the courtesy of more time. In this case, you're looking for a reason to delay the final verdict. Anything you can do to push the decision into the future will help defuse the emotional need to bring the matter to a sudden and perhaps unfortunate conclusion. Just as important, more time will give you an opportunity to find out more about the motivation and intentions of those who may be working against you, or perhaps, working on behalf of someone else. Use the same delaying strategy we discussed before, rationalizing your request with the need to research or confirm some aspects of the topic, especially the circumstances influencing management's predisposition. If necessary, stress the importance of making an objective and informed decision—something you both want.

Chapter Fourteen
Use Ethical Manipulation to Work Your Way to the Top

We typically associate the word *manipulation* with coercion or exploitation. There's often the implication of controlling or forcing someone to do something they wouldn't ordinarily want to do.

That's one definition.

Here's another, and this is the one that counts: Using your communication skills to persuade and influence others.

Persuading and influencing have always been recognized as important aspects of selling. And since we spend most of our time trying to sell something to someone—for example, coaxing our spouse into trying a new Mexican food restaurant, encouraging our teenage daughter to give up smoking, or convincing our boss we're worth every bit of an eight percent raise instead of five—we're constantly involved in persuading and influencing.

In a business context, using a strategy of persuasion and influence can be extremely powerful, especially when you need to make an impact on those who have the authority to make a difference in your career.

But here's the problem: Most of us use only a fraction of our ability to influence others. This is especially true when we communicate our thoughts and desires in a way that makes them difficult to understand. If we want others to make a difference in our favor, we need to consider their preferred method of receiving input from the outside world. And that often means using more than our vocabulary.

Our goal is to improve our communication with others by conveying ideas and concepts with less vagueness or confusion.

Essentially, it's tailoring your delivery to match the way others want to receive it.

The first step is to determine how an individual processes information, especially when making decisions. For example, when the boss comes to a positive conclusion, does she usually jump to the endgame and then look back to determine the necessary steps it took to get there? If so, your presentation should paint a picture of what you want to accomplish in its final form, complete with its associated features and benefits. Then offer a concise review of the activities required to accomplish it. In other words, if the person you're trying to convince wants to hear about the bottom line *first*—the result, advantages, and benefits—then evaluate the cost based on the steps necessary to achieve it, that's the way to make your presentation.

If this sounds illogical or complicated, it's because you're not used to doing it that way. You may be so accustomed to using a single channel of delivery—based on your own preferences of how you describe the world around you—that you've assumed it's also the way everyone else processes what they see, hear, and feel. Your method of presenting thoughts and ideas may be sensible, logical, and straightforward *for you*, but it may not be the ideal method for your listener, especially if you want them to agree with you.

Let's go back to our example of the boss who automatically jumps to the endgame and then looks back on what it took to get there.

If you ignore this individual's preferred method of processing information and take the reverse approach—first describing all the details necessary to plan, prepare, and execute the steps to accomplish the end-goal, then reveal the bottom-line payoff as your big finish—she'll become bored, anxious, or indifferent. She may even say something like, "I don't think we're speaking the same language."

The key to effective communication is to match the preferred modalities of your listener. And before you dismiss this idea as overly complicated or too involved, you should know that by making just a few adjustments, you often become easier to understand, and your ideas earn greater credibility—*by that specific individual.*

Adjusting the order of your presentation is only one variable that can improve your communication skills. Here's a couple more:

- **Adjust the rate of your speech.** How fast does the other person usually speak? Do the words pour from their mouth at a machine-gun rate? Or do they speak slowly, purposely, pausing between words and sentences to give weight and authority to each thought? Matching your rate of speech to that of the listener will typically result in better rapport and increased understanding. And here's a real bonus: You'll often be considered more intelligent by that individual!

- **Match their primary representational system.** Listen to the specific words they commonly use. If you're listening to someone who is in "visual mode," you'll typically hear words and phrases like, *it's clear, bright, I see, take a look, I can't see myself doing that, it's just too dark to go there,* and other visually-oriented words (called predicates).

On the other hand, someone who is more of an "auditory" is sensitive to the sound of the spoken word. They're listening and processing information from the pitch and tonality of the speaker. They use phrases like, *I hear you, it's clear as a bell, it's whisper-quiet down here, listen to this, it sounds like,* and so on.

The third "type" of representational systems is called kinesthetic," referring to those who usually process conversation by developing a feeling about the subject. These folks *need to get a handle on things, touch base, will tell you it doesn't feel right, it's not comfortable, may want to take it out for a spin, run it up the flagpole, get their hands around it,* and so on.

Avoid making the mistake of labeling anyone a permanent visual, auditory, or kinesthetic. An individual's representational system can change quickly, based on the subject and the environment. But if you listen intently and identify the primary predicates being used, you can determine how your listener is processing information *at that time*, and then match the representation system they're using. How will you know if and when you're in sync with your listener? Both of you will get the *sense* that you're *on the same page.* Get it?

These suggestions are derived from Neuro-linguistic Programming (NLP) and are simple processes that can be used to quickly establish rapport with others. While there are lots of books available about NLP, an in-person learning experience with lots of practice sessions is the best way to master the technology. If you want to know more about NLP and how to use it effectively, do an online search to find a weekend class or seminar.

Chapter Fifteen
Networking

Attending company-sponsored events, seminars, conventions, and conferences are an integral part of working for the man. Yes, the expanded use of video and teleconferencing technology has created a strong financial argument against in-person meetings. But managers also know the value of the added synergy resulting from meeting company executives and co-workers face-to-face. So unless the organization is in a cash-flow crunch, you can expect the process of pressing the flesh to continue.

Make it a priority to use these get-togethers to your advantage. You may have talked to John Smith a dozen times on the phone, but chatting with John in person brings a different dynamic to the relationship. Your job is to make sure your face-to-face exchange enhances John's opinion of you.

Make no mistake about why you're there. While the atmosphere typically provides plenty of opportunities to socialize, it's still a business function, and there are always lots of eyes on you. Don't screw up your chances for promotion by letting your hair down, drinking a pitcher of Margaritas, then convincing the secretary to go skinny dipping with you in the hotel pool. (Yep, saw it happen.)

Your goal should be to meet as many new people as possible, some of which may have the potential to boost your career or provide valuable inside information that would otherwise be unavailable to you. Here's a quick tutorial on the best ways to strike up a conversation with a stranger.

Extend an unmistakable welcome. We tend to avoid those we don't know, but the usual social conventions that restrict our interaction with strangers are not as stringent at a business-sponsored event. Try saying "hello" to someone when standing in line, while in an elevator, while waiting for a presentation to begin, or wherever you encounter someone you don't know and innocent chit-chat is acceptable. The stranger in the elevator may turn out to be the VP of marketing, but if you don't make the first move to break the ice, you'll never know.

What if you don't know how to chit-chat? Here's how it's done. Let's begin by identifying the players. You're "A." The stranger is "B." Your focus is on "C." Your initial comment or question is always about "C," meaning you pick a subject that does not involve you or the stranger. It might be the food, a positive comment about the day, the weather, or the color of a shirt *someone else* is wearing. Never begin by complimenting the stranger's appearance. It not only sends up a red flag, it can leave you without a comfortable transition in conversation.

Try to choose a topic that both of you have in common. For example, forgetting an umbrella when it's pouring outside, praising the presenter's skills in a seminar you both attended, or a comment about the food or venue. Just be yourself and if you receive a friendly response, continue the conversation by asking a question or two.

If you're part of a group within the same industry or company, it's okay to use that mutual relationship as the "C." For example, "How long have you been with Acme Corporation?" Or, "This is my first national convention. How about you?"

To be a productive "networker," you'll spend most of your time doing two things: listening and talking. Make sure it's in that order, preferably in a ratio of about 80/20. Be a great listener, and you'll make a great impression. People love to talk about themselves. Your job is to listen attentively, ask questions, and provide positive feedback.

Always use discretion when revealing personal information to someone you just met. Just because the other person is extremely forthcoming with personal or even intimate details, don't feel obligated to do the same. We typically make assumptions about others during our initial meeting, and revealing too much, too soon, can send the wrong impression. For example, if you spill your guts about your wife's affair with the gardener, you'll probably end up regretting it.

Keep your conversation positive and upbeat. If the new acquaintance begins to rant about problems at work or home, listen politely, but don't agree with his argument or reinforce his opinion if it means taking sides. When you've had enough, nod and say, "You'll have to excuse me, but a co-worker is flagging me, and I need to check in with her. I wish you the best with that situation, and I hope it works out well for you."

Avoid trying to elicit comments by wearing something odd or unusual. It may influence or "taint" a stranger's opinion of you before you can say a single word. And yes, men, this includes gaudy ties (I remember some guy wearing a bright yellow tie with a big, red fish to a job interview. That wasn't the reason I didn't hire him, but I couldn't stop thinking about that stupid tie.)

Here are several more suggestions you can use to strike up a conversation and establish rapport:

• **Quickly smile and say, "Hi."** This is the easiest way to approach and completely disarm someone. They're seldom expecting it, and it opens a door that lets the conversation flow. *However, timing is critical.* You *must* smile and get the "hi" out of your mouth in the very first second of the encounter, or it won't have the same impact. And only use the word "Hi." Saying *Hello, how are you*, or some other form of greeting, won't work as well. Follow it up with a comment about something in the immediate vicinity, (using the A-B-C method), and in twenty seconds you'll be talking like old friends.

- **Match eye contact.** I've heard personal communication experts suggest looking directly into a stranger's eyes when talking to them. However, too much eye contact can backfire and make others feel "stare-conscious," resulting in them feeling nervous or uncomfortable. The key is to *match* their eye-to-eye time. If they appear to have trouble looking directly at you, try glancing away every now and then, allowing them to evaluate you without pressure.

- **Listen to other conversations.** Be aware of what's going on around you. If you pick up on something interesting, simply approach the person and say, "I couldn't help overhearing your comments about . . ." Then take it from there.

- **Create an "elevator pitch."** The opportunity to meet someone new is often constrained by time limits (and thus was born the "elevator pitch"). In these spontaneous situations, you typically have less than a minute to make a positive impression. The goal is to leave your new acquaintance with a clear indication of who you are and what you do—especially when your intention is to make a new business contact.

A friend of mine piques the interest of strangers who ask him what he does for a living by saying, "*I'm a fixer.*" You can imagine the questions he receives, which allows him to fashion his response and personalize the conversation to his advantage.

Avoid "techno-speak." There's no faster way to distance yourself from others than by using a string of industry-specific words and phrases that leaves laypeople and generalists with only a vague understanding of what you're saying. Common sense suggests using clear, concise language while avoiding vague or confusing terms and phrases—because no one wants to use a dictionary after meeting you to try to figure out what you said.

Unfortunately, I frequently overhear introductions and first-time meetings brimming with techno-speak, and from the aftermath of negative body language and blank expressions, the resulting lack of clarity has left one of the parties unsure about the value of any future contact.

Using rhetoric that sounds like a third-party description can put distance between you and your listener. It can also make you seem detached, impersonal, and even a little arrogant. Someone who might have presented you with a new business opportunity may decide you're full of BS and immediately discount your talent and ability.

Adopting the vocabulary of your chosen field is a necessary and expected part of any profession. It's often a shortcut to understanding and communicating with others who are proficient in the specialized jargon of your industry. However, knowing when to use it, and when to translate it into lay-speak, is vital in creating positive first impressions, especially when you're trying to establish credibility and authenticity.

Here's how to translate *high-tech* vocabulary into *human-speak*. It's based on a three-step method I've used for years, and I often recommend it to technical salespeople, engineers, and other "techies" when introducing themselves to strangers. (Excerpted from *Speak Up! A Step-by-Step Method to Conquer Your Fears and Give an Amazing Speech*, by yours truly.)

First, describe what you do in layman's terms. Instead of introducing yourself as a Systems and Procedural Auditing Consultant, explain that you work in the accounting industry, consulting with medium to large businesses to identify wasteful and redundant spending while implementing effective tax strategies and improving profitability.

Use a *brief* story to explain your work in terms of its benefit to your clients. Staying with our accountant example, it might sound like this: "I recently saved a client tens of thousands of dollars annually by comparing the economic advantages of selling his storefront to an investor and leasing it back versus personal ownership."

If your listener is still interested (based on their verbal and non-verbal feedback), invite them to contact you with questions or if they encounter a situation in which your input could prove useful. Unless your time or services are extremely limited—for example, you have a two-year waiting list of potential clients—make it clear that the initial call is complimentary. Emphasizing your availability with something like, "let me know if I can help," can also be extremely effective.

Leave others with a positive impression. Yes, first impressions are important, and so are *exit* impressions. We tend to dismiss the importance of the exit because we think it's the normal result of our conversation coming to a close. However, just like the process of initiating a conversation, the exit can be structured, formatted, and delivered in a way that leaves others wanting to follow up and make future contact.

Try using a few phrases that bring your interchange to a comfortable conclusion. For example, "I've really enjoyed chatting with you. I hope we can continue our conversation later in the week (or whenever would be the next appropriate time). Or, "Your thoughts and ideas on (the subject under discussion) are very interesting. I'd like to hear more. Maybe we can get together next week for lunch?"

Depending on the circumstances, you can also try a more personalized exit. For example, "Thanks so much for the conversation. I almost didn't come to the luncheon, but I'm really glad I did."

Invite future contact. This can be nothing more than an exchange of business cards, or a cell-phone "hot-swap" (NFC – near field communication) of phone numbers and email.

What if you meet someone who wants to argue about everything? I know there's plenty of lawyers and debate teachers who believe the practice of arguing is nothing more than pursuing a logical and protracted discussion of evidence, opinion, and circumstance. (And they're willing to argue the point until way past my bedtime.) In some circles, it's thought to be a legitimate tool of getting to a better answer, to generate new ideas, and motivate new thinking that would not otherwise happen.

My advice? Treat an argument like the plague.

Engaging in an argument is an outright challenge, the verbal equivalent of throwing down the gauntlet. It says, I'm right and you're wrong, and nothing you can say is going to change my mind.

I used to engage in arguments, believing others would never respect my opinions unless I verbally defended them. Even when the subject or the outcome was of little value, I made sure the other side knew precisely how I felt and why. I finally realized how much time I was wasting—and how many bridges I was burning.

In the working world—a place where progress is measured in productivity and positive relationships—there's a big difference between a discussion and an argument. Here are the most critical distinctions:

- The majority of arguments are a waste of time. Seldom does either party accomplish anything, and it's rare that one person changes the mind of the other. When people feel challenged or threatened, they typically dig their heels in deeper and fight even harder to maintain their sense of identity, authority, and personal power.

- Many arguments are fueled by the need for personal recognition, often giving voice to those who otherwise have nothing to say. Contrary to those who believe they can overwhelm and overcome any opponent with their logic and well-structured rhetoric, argument it's a poor technique for demonstrating intelligence. Habitually argumentative people are often seen by others as belligerent, arrogant, and difficult. The result? No one wants to be around them.

• Compared to an argument, a *discussion* is a civil, respectful exchange of ideas, opinions, and intentions. Points of potential disagreement are often presented as questions, needing clarification. The goal is to understand the other side's needs. By asking for more information, both sides arrive at reasons to see the situation more clearly. Even if your antagonist does not ultimately agree with you, they are far more likely to respect you for your reasonable approach to the subject, and the fact you were willing to listen. If your intention is to motivate others to objectively consider your side of the issue before making a final decision, learning to use the nuances of a directed discussion can be very effective in reaching your goals.

How do you diffuse a potential argument? Here are a few suggestions on how to move from a potentially volatile dispute to an amicable discussion:

1. Determine the importance of the subject. Then set limits on your responses, attitude, and general behavior. Is insisting the other person understand or even agree with your position worth losing any future association with them? If you have an existing personal or business relationship with someone, don't put that relationship at risk over subjects that are insignificant or unimportant.

2. **Never argue opinion.** Most strongly-held beliefs are nothing more than personal opinions. I've heard heated arguments over which lake has better fishing potential, or which guitarist is more talented, or which singer has the better voice. No two people evaluate the same situation in exactly the same

way. Allow others to express their opinion without the need to respond with judgment. It's an essential requirement for maintaining rapport and deriving future benefit from the relationship.

3. **Make an intentional effort to LISTEN.** Ask questions. If you truly don't understand the other person's logic, ask for an example. It's an indication you're trying to see their point of view. Most will appreciate your objective mindset.

4. **Never lose your temper.** Maintain your focus on what's important. If the other person becomes emotional or childish, see the situation for what it is: a desperate cry for personal validation. The phrase "for the sake of argument," describes an immature and self-indulgent approach to communicating with others.

5. **Create space for the other person to be right.** Instead of pronouncing an idea or opinion wrong, use language that suggests the existence of alternatives that could be equally accurate. Phrases such as, "I wonder if . . ." or "I've always thought there might be more to the subject, so my opinion is still in the formative stages."

6. **Respect the other person's viewpoint by bestowing their thoughts with credibility.** Use a phrase like, "That's an interesting viewpoint; I hadn't thought of it that way." You're not saying you agree with them, but you're not outright dismissing them, either.

7. **Reduce the use of the word "but" from your vocabulary.** When you use the word *but*, everything said immediately prior is disputed or at least discounted. It's inherently argumentative and dismissive. Try using the word "and" in its place and see what happens. It may seem awkward at first, but if you don't hesitate or place undue emphasis when making the replacement, you'll be surprised at how effective this

simple technique can be at lowering the defenses of others and enhancing your communication in general.

8. **Don't allow others to bully you verbally.** If you find yourself confronted with an argumentative person who wants to "show you who's boss," or insists on using an argumentative stance to bring attention to himself while in the presence of others, try changing the subject. If that doesn't work, excuse yourself with a prior commitment. You don't need to wait for an opening in the flow of rhetoric because you may not get one. Simply say, *"That sounds interesting, and I'm sorry I can't stay, but I'm running late for my next appointment, so I have to say goodbye. Perhaps we can continue our discussion at another time."* Then smile and walk away.

I'll end this section on networking with this: Honing your social skills will get you noticed and on the shortlist for promotion. Communicating on paper is essential, but being able to share your thoughts and ideas face-to-face is the hallmark of a leader. If you're serious about your career, it's not something you can leave to chance. Like any other skill, in-person communication is an ability that can be developed and improved with preparation and practice.

Chapter Sixteen
Takeovers, Buyouts, Divisionalization, and Reorganization

No matter what it's called, it's a nasty process, and it usually means *heads will roll!*

From the moment your company becomes involved in one of these situations, there's the very real possibility your job will soon be in jeopardy, regardless of how valued an employee you've been.

It often starts as a rumor—a large conglomerate is looking to acquire a stake in a new market, and your company is a prime candidate.

"But wait! The company I work for isn't for sale," you say.

Is the stock publicly traded? If so, it's always for sale. For example, a personal or institutional shareholder might decide to sell a substantial block of stock, resulting in the buyer's new cumulative equity equating to a majority position. Alternatively, in a bid for ownership, a buyer may issue a blanket offer to purchase shares from existing stockholders. Even owners of privately held companies can decide to abandon ship and sell to the highest bidder, tempted by a large payday and the lure of a well-funded retirement.

If the buyer is a larger company, your future is especially tenuous, since your company will typically be absorbed and end up as a division of the larger organization—or worse, your company's core assets will be dissected and selectively incorporated into the buyer's current line of products and services, with the left-overs discarded as unwanted scrap.

What does it mean to you and your career? You may have spent years proving yourself, forming positive relationships with upper-level management, and winning the respect of your co-workers, but none of it matters now. Regardless of what the acquiring company's management initially tells you, your career, livelihood, and lifestyle are on the line. And until you have successfully navigated the transition and reorganization phase, your future is uncertain at best.

Even if you're asked to stay or you retain your job by default, you may feel as if you're being forced to start over (in some cases, you are), with little to no recognition for the part you played in the company's past success.

There is always a timeline for the transition. When the buyout or acquisition is friendly (occurring between a willing buyer and an agreeable seller), the result is typically business as usual—for a while. The acquiring company may leave its new purchase alone for a year or two, using the time to learn more about the internal operation and the functions of key management personnel.

However, if it's a hostile take-over, the timeline can accelerate, making your future an uncertain mix of down-sizing, cut-backs, and layoffs as duplicated management and job functions are eliminated in bulk. Although the process seldom takes place overnight, the goals and agenda of the acquiring company are typically structured like this:

- Sell off or close unprofitable divisions.
- Restructure and streamline management.
- Re-assign, demote, or layoff excess and redundant workers and terminate undesirable employees.

The above list is not in order of priority. Management could just as easily begin the reorganization in reverse order.

During this period of transition, the new owner typically reviews employee assignments and job functions to determine the most effective and profitable method of managing the acquired company's workforce. Many of the decisions concerning who ultimately keeps their job and who is shown the door will be based on the prime assets that motivated the purchase. In other words, if the new owner wanted the company's manufacturing capability, but doesn't need a sales force—*and you work in sales*—there's an overwhelming likelihood that you'll either be terminated or managed out.

This leaves one big question:

If your job is one of those considered expendable, how long do you have before you can expect to receive a notice of termination?

The larger the company you work for, the more time is typically needed to implement management transitions while mitigating termination liability. Unfortunately, it's during these longer-term transitions that professional relationships can become toxic, if not outright hostile. The result is a potentially terminal situation for the careers of Loyalists and Users alike.

In a worse-case situation, the process can go on for several years, meaning the suspicion, back-stabbing, and name-calling can continue—and escalate—until new management implements its final decisions.

Knowing your job is in jeopardy can be one of the most stressful, frustrating times of your life. The comfortable familiarity of people, systems, and procedures are turned upside down. And the sense of security you had—even though you knew there was always the possibility it could change—is gone.

But this is not the time to feel sorry for yourself. Your time-window for action is both limited and critical.

At the earliest opportunity, let new management know of your past loyalty, your welcoming acceptance of their influence, and how much you're looking forward to the benefits and advantages their stewardship brings to your future. Then emphasize your desire to continue to do your best work under the new flag of ownership.

Sound like brown-nosing? It isn't. It's a forthright disclosure of your intentions and what management can expect from you during the transition. Just as important, it demonstrates your professional response to the changed situation. If you feel your pride or ego getting in the way, just remind yourself how powerful this simple strategy can be in removing your name from the top of the termination list. In fact, it could be the very thing that influences the decision-makers to keep you in your current job or offer you a new position in another branch or division.

So do it whether you mean it or not!

During the transition, the new management's priority is to maintain the *external* status quo—the existing customers, gross sales, and market share of the company—with as little disruption to the bottom line as possible. Your new supervisor will evaluate you and your job function based on the company's current needs, not on their future plans for expansion. The assessment of inherited employees is an on-going and evolving process, with the priority focused on finding the most expedient and profitable way to incorporate the newly acquired business into the larger financial picture.

This is not a good time to originate a request for a transfer to the sales office in Hawaii or ask for a move from the marketing division to fleet management. If you're offered a transfer or relocation, it will originate from the new owner's evaluation of the marketplace—not from a need to placate your personal need for a change in scenery.

The exception? If you discover your job function is being eliminated or is going to be assumed by someone else, you have nothing to lose. Just keep in mind that asking for a transfer during reorganization can move you closer to the top of the termination list.

Let's take a closer look at the process of reorganization. First, make no mistake; those who have the responsibility of making a final decision about your future with the company will make it without any consideration of how it will affect your life and livelihood—*because the retention of their job depends on it!* Their priority is on self-survival, and so must yours.

While the tactics of "managing out" can range from mild manipulation to well-planned, underhanded schemes and ploys, the worst abuses occur when the acquired company is top-heavy with duplicate-function employees.

Competing managers are especially at risk following a buyout. Reassigning, demoting, or terminating duplicate managers—those whose job will be taken over by a manager from the parent company—is usually completed before restructuring the subordinate employee workforce. While some redundant supervisors may be absorbed into the new company structure, others will be offered early retirement or a down-graded position, primarily to avoid a wrongful termination or discrimination lawsuit. Early retirement or "alternative positioning" is more likely if the employee is near the age of retirement or belongs to a minority. However, don't' count on your age, seniority, or protected class to make you bulletproof. Managers who don't demonstrate their receptivity to relocate, transfer, or accept a new assignment, are usually terminated.

Your enemy is not always obvious. There is real danger in believing that "alien" managers—those not working within your division, or who are employed by a seemingly unassociated part of the acquiring company—have no power over you. If you find yourself having correspondence with them, it's a dead giveaway they have the potential to wreak their special brand of havoc on your future.

Here's another tipoff: If they choose to meet with you personally, you're definitely talking to someone who can make or break your career. Their need for a face-to-face meeting is not an accident. They're on a mission, and their objective may be to eliminate your future with the company. (Overly dramatic? Ask any mid-level manager who has been the victim of a takeover or buyout.)

If you find yourself in this situation, you need to protect your career with a contingency plan. Timing is everything. *When* you implement your plan is based on how much time remains before your job function—*and you*—are evaluated and possibly eliminated. Unfortunately, your manager or the HR department is seldom going to provide you with an actual date. Sometimes, the best you can do is to monitor the "hostility index" by watching for the subtle and not-so-subtle signs that typically indicate a major change is waiting for you right outside your door.

The most obvious red flag is the baiting of subordinates. This is a down and dirty tactic used by opposing managers of equal position and rank. The idea is to purposely bait the subordinates of the other manager with innuendo and sometimes outright false accusations of improper conduct, invented inadequacies, or claims of incompetence. The worst of the snakes—the "little Caesars" of the acquiring company—are seldom satisfied to merely suggest their poisonous message and will express it outright, in public, and without regard to who hears it.

Here are two examples I've personally heard:

- "After my people take over, things will run a lot smoother. And they'll do the job with fewer mistakes and greater effectiveness."

- "My team wouldn't have created such a mess out of things."

Your best defense? Sometimes there isn't any, especially if your termination date is already scrawled on your new manager's calendar. But if your future has yet to be determined, here's some advice to buy time until you learn more about your options or can find another job.

1. **Practice careful silence.** The intention of a "little Caesar" is to provoke you to the point that you lose control or behave in an unprofessional manner, especially in front of others. He wants witnesses, preferably other employees, to see it happen. He will insult, incite, and aggravate you, hoping you'll fly off the handle. And if he can get you to threaten him with retribution or even physical violence, so much the better—for him. For example, returning his bullying and harassment with, "If you keep accusing me of this kind of crap, I'm going to take you outside and kick your ass," will make his day. (By the way, while I'm the first one to say that most little Caesars deserve a good ass-kicking, threatening to deliver one will hurt *you*, not the other way around.)

Remember, threats of physical violence—even if delivered as a vague suggestion—is one of the few justifications a company needs to terminate you immediately without recourse. And it's exactly what a little Caesar is looking for; a way to get rid of as many inherited employees as possible and replace them with *his* people.

2. **Demonstrate discipline and professionalism under fire.** This is the exact opposite of what your opponent is hoping for. Even better, it usually makes a little Cesar look like an idiot. Try saying something like, "I've heard a lot of false accusations disguised as innuendo, and it's unfortunate and troubling to hear. It undermines the morale of our employees and reflects

poorly on the reputation of those who repeat it. Personally, I've made it a point to avoid responding to it."

Keep in mind that the worse possible outcome of a confrontation with a Little Caesar is to have him become your new boss. If that turns out to be your fate, there's a good chance he knew of your eventual transfer to his authority and was building his file of evidence to substantiate his future decision to terminate you.

3. **Update your resume and call a headhunter**. Let them know you're available and ready to leave your current employer. When asked about your reason for leaving, say the recent changes within your company have prompted you to look at other opportunities. Then add that while you've been assured by the new management they want you to continue in your current position while waiting for a promotion, you feel it's a good time to consider all the options. Then add, "In fact, the changes taking place within the company couldn't have come at a better time, since I've been thinking about reassessing my career path for several months."

This kind of sales pitch helps the headhunter market your qualifications to companies that may express concerns about negative industry rumors surrounding the company's recent acquisition or reorganization.

By the way, trying to convince a headhunter that the changes going on in your company are minor or have nothing to do with your desire to seek other employment is seldom productive. They know what's going on. And while you shouldn't reveal the possibility that you're about to be terminated, there's no advantage in suggesting the takeover hasn't influenced your decision to look for new career opportunities.

Again, the sooner you start looking, the better. Your former industry competitors are now prospective employers. They expect employee fall-out from the transition, and they're primed to grab the best and most talented.

Waiting to begin your job search until *after* you're terminated will put you at a definite disadvantage. At that point, employers will interpret your availability as a personal need to replace your last job instead of a desire to improve your career in the long-term.

If there's ever a time to put you and your career first, this is it. If you've decided it's in your best interest to leave, buy yourself as much time as possible. If necessary, agree to a demotion or re-assignment to maintain your income while you look for another job. You're much more "hire-able" when employed.

Wait! What if you're not ready to leave? If you know for a fact that you're not on the list of expendable employees, finding your place within the new or reorganized company can have its benefits. The acquiring company (which we'll call "Megacorp") may offer more opportunities for advancement, perhaps even the chance to work in a completely different field or industry.

If Megacorp provides you with assurances of your continued employment—either by written contract, promotion, or with an expenditure of money to accommodate your retention through relocation or training—revisit your list of values and priorities established when evaluating the company's original job offer. Your motivations may have changed (matured?). You may also find it helpful to re-define which items are now negotiable and which are not. Things like your self-respect, identity, and credibility will no doubt remain as high priorities. Items moving to the negotiable side of the list might include things like the amount of travel that's acceptable, relocation to another part of the country, or reassignment to a different division of the company.

Once you're committed to staying through the transition and beyond, learn as much as you can about the structure, the products, and management of Megacorp. The identity of your old company—its autonomy, chain of authority, procedures, and policies—are gone now, so you must reshape yourself into an employee of Megacorp.

Develop a game plan. Start by determining and prioritizing your customer's concerns originating from the takeover and develop a plan to alleviate them. Share this plan with your boss. Focus on how to reduce and eliminate problems with brand conversion and confusion over who's responsible for what under the new regime.

After the fallout from the reorganization has settled, you can begin looking for new opportunities. For example, if you've worked in sales for the last ten years and you're ready for a change, take a look at marketing, advertising, asset management, or human resources.

When making comparisons of compensation, workload, and probable longevity, make sure the new position is an unlikely candidate for outsourcing. Then consider the possibilities for advancement. Is it a dead-end job? Or a grooming station for new vice-presidents?

Loyalty during a takeover or re-organization . . . to the boss, your co-workers, and to yourself. This is a tough one. And the "right" way of handling it is not always obvious. Here's a true story to illustrate my point:

After Mega-Corp completed the financial and legal aspects of buying Acme Corporation, I received a call from a former Acme division head—at least that's who he claimed to be. He said he was based out of the corporate headquarters, and yet, after working for thirteen years at Acme, I'd never heard of him. However, he mentioned several names I did know, and with every word, his voice assumed an increasing sense of authority and urgency. He made it clear he wasn't calling to chat about the weather and wanted to get right down to business.

"What do you think of your boss?" he asked.

"Great guy," I answered. "Does a good job. Always there when I need him, and he shoots straight from the hip."

"But there's certainly room for improvement, right? He asked. "Aren't there times when he could provide more direction and better feedback?

Something was up. Under normal circumstances, these kinds of questions would never be asked of a subordinate. The only exceptions would involve evidence of impropriety, illegal activity, or the decision to terminate my boss had been made, and I was being considered as a candidate for his replacement.

I was fairly sure none of those things were likely.

The caller's innuendo—centered squarely on my boss—soon turned into a flow of outright accusations of ineffective management. Despite his insistence that I confirm his allegations, I refused to agree with him. Using as many instances as I could think of, I related examples of my supervisor's successful handling of competitive situations and politically sensitive circumstances between customers and the company.

I ended the conversation by saying I enjoyed working for my current supervisor, thought very highly of him, and supported him one hundred percent.

After hanging up, my next call was to the LA sales office. As soon as I had my boss on the phone, I told him everything.

"He was on a witch-hunt," I said. "I don't know who you pissed off, but this guy is looking for a reason to can your ass."

My boss, (we'll call him Mr. Snook) was quiet for a moment, then said, "I'd planned on telling you this during my next visit to Phoenix, but it sounds like things are moving faster than I'd anticipated. A couple of months ago, I was told to find a way to terminate you. Since your sales performance has always been outstanding and you've made a lot of money for the company, I asked for a specific reason. The regional manager said your performance didn't have anything to do with it. He said you weren't a team player and he had no use for you."

Mr. Snook paused, waiting for me to say something.

"What else?" I asked. I was having a hard time believing my career was about to be trashed because of a personal vendetta, so I assumed there was more to the story.

"I told him I didn't have any reason to fire you," Snook continued. "And if he wanted it done, he'd have to do it himself. However, I warned him there was a good possibility you'd take a large percentage of the business with you because of your long term relationship with your customers."

"You think that's why the guy from corporate called me? I asked. "To see if I'd say something negative about you, so you'd have a reason to get rid of me?"

"I don't know. But I'm sure it has something to do with my refusal to let you go. Maybe the guy thinks we've formed a pact for mutual protection—you cover my ass, I cover yours, that kind of thing. It's the only reason I can think of that would explain those kinds of questions."

We ended the call with a mutual promise to advise each other of any follow-up calls from witch-hunters. We both knew that was unlikely. I'd failed to bite, refusing to give management what they wanted. From then on, I would be considered an uncooperative rebel—at the top of the list of expendable employees.

I thought about that phone call from headquarters for a long time. I was sure the caller's accusations were manufactured for political reasons. My boss was a good manager. He'd been with the company for over twenty years, and while his management style didn't reflect the polished gleam of a Harvard MBA (on occasion, he could be blunt and uncompromising), he was honest and fair. And unlike some of the managers I'd met from other regions, his objectives were well defined and easy to understand. He made it clear what he expected, how my performance would be measured, and as long as my numbers were good, he left me alone.

For me, he was the perfect boss.

But for the sake of argument, let's flip the situation and take another look at the loyalty question. What if the relationship with my boss had been fraught with problems? What if he'd made my life miserable with endless demands to change the way I did things? Or saddled me with a constant schedule of out of town training assignments that doubled my travel time?

My response to the witch-hunter would have been the same.

Why not throw my boss under the bus when I had the chance? I had no idea who the witch-hunter really was, or what he planned to do with the information he was asking for. He could have been recording our conversation, planning to share my responses with management, which could have included my boss. By disparaging my supervisor, I would have substantiated the regional manager's claim that I wasn't a team player, providing Mr. Regional with the ammunition he needed to show me the door.

Regardless of how you feel about your boss personally, you must respect the hierarchy and the structure of command—if you want to keep your job. A subordinate is expected to protect the boss until that boss is replaced. It's part of your responsibility.

If you find yourself in this situation, try to buy some time. When someone contacts you by phone and is obviously looking for dirt, they're hoping to catch you off-guard. They're also assuming a straightforward approach will lower your defenses. The caller is being honest and candid, so it's only logical for you to do the same, right?

Thankfully, these situations rarely take place face to face. It's too incriminating for the instigator. So use the phone to your advantage. Allow the caller to talk long enough to find out their purpose and intentions, then apologize and tell them that someone just walked into your office and you can't speak freely. Set a time to return the call, and in the interim, contact your supervisor and ask them if they know what's going on and how you should respond.

Questions originating from an unfamiliar source that concerns another employee's productivity, skill, or dedication—regardless of whether it's an equal or a supervisor—should be delayed until you can find out what's really going on. You owe your allegiance to your boss and co-workers, not to some stranger who calls you out of the blue. Even if you're later accused of protecting an incompetent superior by putting up a smokescreen, you'll be respected for your loyalty.

The best advice I received during Mega-corp's takeover of Acme came from a mentor, friend, and former boss, Bob Doty, the then Vice President of Furnas Corporation. He told me, "Keep your eyes and ears open, protect yourself, and always look for the opportunity."

In most takeover situations, relinquishing your economic and professional future to a new set of managers—*and hoping everything will eventually work out for the best*—is taking a huge gamble with your career. Rather than adopting an attitude of complacency, be proactive and begin formulating a realistic plan "B." Never forget the most obvious—yet often overlooked—fact of working for someone else: No one will have more of a vested interest in your long-term success than you.

Chapter Seventeen
The Most Dangerous Enemies to a Successful Corporate Career

Negotiating your way through the political and bureaucratic landscape of a typical corporation can be challenging, but regardless of how intense the battle or how overwhelming the odds, the two biggest adversaries you're likely to encounter will be ones you'd least expect . . .

Ego and Complacency.

None of us are immune. Although you seldom hear these behavioral landmines mentioned as reasons for termination, they end as many careers as any other symptom associated with poor performance.

So why are ego and complacency so destructive? Because they're built into our psyche, and if we don't actively manage their influence, they can overwhelm the best of intentions, effectively sabotaging what could have been a successful career.

Let's take *ego* first. It's no secret we want to be recognized for what we do. We need that sense of acknowledgment that comes from performing well, from accomplishing something of value, and from making a difference.

How important is that acknowledgment? The lack of it is often cited as a reason for leaving an otherwise good job. In fact, the mental boost that comes from receiving acknowledgment and praise can be just as important as the money and other economic benefits workers receive as traditional compensation—and employers are finally beginning to realize it.

And that's good. But don't forget—it's a two-way street.

Your manager also has an ego.

So while you're waiting for recognition, expecting praise for what you believe is a job well done, *your manager also needs to be appreciated.*

She's no different than you are. She wants to be acknowledged for doing a good job, for making sacrifices for the good of the team, for providing you with access to her experience and knowledge.

And yet, how often do employees thank their manager when the situation calls for it?

Much too rarely.

And it's not because we've forgotten our manners, or we've chosen to be intentionally rude. It's the result of putting *our* ego first. We're often so self-absorbed that we're oblivious to the needs of others.

Requiring constant validation of our value and contribution will be perceived as is an indication of professional immaturity. Yes, we all want it, but wearing a sign on our back that says, "Compliment me on a regular basis," sends the wrong message—especially to management.

So how do you neutralize your ego? First, realize that the symptoms of a self-destructive ego can range from bragging and calling attention to yourself and your accomplishments, to more serious indicators, such as dependency, being needy, or self-centered entitlement—all of which can be ultimately fatal to your career.

From a management perspective, responsibility and dependency are diametric opposites. Want more responsibility and the rewards that come with it? Show management you have the confidence and self-reliance to handle it. Your actions and behavior must broadcast a level of professionalism that others will aspire to.

Here's the secret about ego (and the stroking thereof):

Ego is a game. And if you learn how to play, you can dramatically increase your influence, perceived competence, and likeability. There are two important rules for playing the game well. The first is to make a point of offering praise and compliments whenever appropriate. The second is to broadcast a positive reaction when receiving approval from others to confirm the commendation is accurate and appropriate.

Let's explore them one at a time.

The first rule is simple and straightforward. Always take advantage of opportunities to compliment a co-worker or supervisor for their accomplishments and successes. And when the glory needs to be shared, be generous to others on your team, acknowledging their contribution and role in getting the job done.

Yes, it's the "right" thing to do, but the real value extends far beyond a display of good protocol. By acknowledging others for their work, you elevate your own value and esteem in the mind of those who receive your compliments. This reverse-logic may seem a bit reaching, but it's real and very powerful. Bottom line, those receiving your compliments will confer you with greater intelligence and credibility because of how correct you are in complimenting them on their performance.

The second part of using ego to your advantage is to make sure your response to receiving praise and recognition compliments the person offering the praise. Your reaction should not only confirm your status as someone who deserves the accolades; it should also validate the giver's decision to bestow them.

Here's a short personal story that illustrates the importance of the second rule:

After several years with Acme, I arrived at the office one morning to find a large package waiting for me. Inside, I found a 24 by 36 inch framed print of an eagle in flight. There was a caption underneath the picture that read, "An Endangered Species." A small engraved brass plate attached to the wood frame contained my name, and underneath, the inscription, "Top Ten Producer."

It was an acknowledgment of my performance and served the same purpose as a trophy or wall plaque.

From the company's perspective, it was tangible recognition of my contribution and was meant to serve as a source of pride.

I saw it as gaudy and pretentious. Every time I looked at it, I felt a tinge of embarrassment. To me, it was . . .

- Verification I was playing their game

- Management's attempt to placate me with a motivational poster

- The presumption that a fifty-dollar poster was all the company thought I was worth

Why did I react with such volatility, especially when it was intended to be a commendation?

The poster was a reminder of the company's failure to live up to their part of the bargain. "More for more," they'd told me, adding, "It's not unusual for our top producers to make more money than their managers."

After eight years on the job, I knew that was false. That year, my boss was making about $135,000[1] (I asked him). By comparison, my W2 was grossing out at about $84,000[1]. If anyone should be making more than their manager, I assumed it would be a top ten producer. But based on the obvious income disparity, those early promises of *more for more* now seemed like a blatant lie.

([1] amount adjusted to 2020 dollars.)

From my cynical perspective, I saw the poster as a consolation prize, a framed note of apology—"Hey, sorry we can't pay you the money we promised, but here's something to appease your ego."

Even worse, I felt cheated—placated with a two-dimensional *image* of success. Not the real thing. To me, it was an embarrassment that screamed, "Loser." Certainly not something that belonged in the office of a successful businessman.

Realizing I was expected to put it on my office wall made my stomach turn. Reluctantly, I hung it in the least conspicuous place I could find. After a month, I took it down and stored it in the maintenance closet. At the end of the year, I threw it out.

Looking back, that was a huge mistake.

Acting out of ego and arrogance, I forgot how important that garish eagle poster was to my boss, and how much it influenced not only him, but those in higher levels of management—all the way up to the president of the company. While it hung on my office wall, they didn't have to check the sales reports to know how I was doing. One look at the poster and they realized I was doing pretty damn well. The award was a visible placeholder, immediately confirming my contribution to the company, and the commensurate level of respect I deserved. In short, it leveled the playing field. I was different from my manager's other subordinates. I had proven myself, and I'd earned the right to exercise greater latitude and independence in how I spent my time on behalf of the company.

What should I have done?

The same thing I advise my readers and listeners to do today. Display the hardware. Take all that wood, brass, and chrome-plated plastic and find a place to show it off. Keep it clean—dust it, polish it, and keep it looking new. Pride of ownership reflects commitment. Your boss will love it, which will influence his evaluation of your work. Every time he walks into your office or cubicle, he'll see your trashy collection of "Atta-boys," and think, "Don't have to worry about Jones. He's a dedicated worker. Takes a lot of pride in what he does."

Here's the bottom line: Companies have learned that the human ego is an easy mark to exploit, often producing greater returns than economic incentives. By using the same strategy, you can maximize the return from your professional relationships, and ultimately, improve your long-term career success. The smart corporate employee doesn't just keep their ego in check, they play the game, using ego as a powerful influence on their managers and co-workers.

What about the other side of the coin . . . Complacency?

Here's the depressing truth: A large percentage of employees allow themselves to become comfortable with the predictability of doing the same job function, over and over, year after year. For these folks, the regularity and (erroneous) certainty of having a consistent income from doing work that has been completely–and often competently—mastered, produces a certain level of "contented" gratification.

Here's the typical mindset of someone who's fallen into the complacency trap:

"Hey, I'm an expert at knocking out these budget proposals. I know the variables and metrics off the top of my head. I've done it for so long, I can do it in my sleep. I always receive recognition for getting it done right and on time. I've got a great thing going, so why would I want to jeopardize it by trying to move up to team leader?"

Now you know the origin of the expression, *"one year of experience, repeated twenty times."*

Even died-in-the-wool *Loyalists* can find their comfort niche. Content in their career and life-work priority, they have no interest in taking on more responsibility. Unless they undergo a significant shift in career priorities, they're satisfied to continue doing their current job for the rest of their working life.

Yes, it's an inviting temptation to settle in and ride it out, knowing you can easily handle whatever the day throws at you. You've got the experience, and you know the ropes. In fact, you've done it so many times, you could direct an assistant to do it while you work on your website, check Facebook, or watch YouTube.

Sound familiar?

Then consider this a wake-up call. You may believe your continued handling of the day-to-day business is sufficient to justify your value and continued employment, but your boss may be wondering how to motivate you, or even worse, she may be wondering if it's too late to reignite the fire.

Supervisors want to see enthusiastic, ambitious employees. It's a source of positive feedback and an indication they're doing a good job as a boss. *Most important, they want to keep those kinds of people around them.*

Does that mean you must constantly strive to move up, to work toward one promotion after another? Absolutely not, especially if you're a *User*, and your real interest—and future— lies beyond your corporate job.

But here's the problem: Regardless of your personal plan and how you see yourself fitting into the company in the long- term, it's important to give management the impression you're a motivated employee. Even if you never move up in job status or position, being seen as ambitious and dedicated are important factors in maintaining your job security. (Okay, let's be honest. No job offers true security, but ambition and dedication—often called "commitment"—can be strong influencers when a supervisor must choose between two otherwise equally qualified employees for termination in the event of a company-wide lay-off.)

Unlike job security, job longevity is not an illusion. Longevity—and the consistent cash flow it represents—is a bankable asset. And while it's seldom within your exclusive control, you *can* influence those who determine the probability of your future employment by increasing your perceived value to management—a definite advantage when layoffs, reorganizations, and managerial turf-wars begin to eliminate less favored employees.

So how do we create the impression of an ambitious, dedicated, and invested employee? First of all, let's make sure we're putting the right perspective on this.

Complacency is a perception.

You may be kicking butt with your numbers and turning in the kind of paperwork that makes the bean-counters weep with joy, but if management doesn't see your name mentioned in a customer's glowing accolades, or hear about your big contract win, they'll assume it's business as usual with you. From their viewpoint, you're merely doing what's necessary, maintaining the status quo.

Does that mean you have to continually work to make a name for yourself? The short answer is "yes." However, don't let this idea overwhelm you—it's much easier to do than it sounds.

First, it isn't necessary to re-invent the wheel, and it's probably better for your career if you don't try.

The key is to give the impression you're broadening the boundaries of your abilities *within* your specific job position—and making sure your manager knows it. One of the best ways of keeping your name at the top of the retention list is to make small enhancements to existing programs and systems that demonstrate your desire to improve (1) gross sales, (2) profit margins, (3) production costs, (4) customer relationships, (5) brand recognition, and (6) employee loyalty. While the specific nature of what you do will depend on your job description and assignment, these six areas represent the highest priorities for most companies.

Remember, your goal is to demonstrate your desire to improve the company's bottom line—*whether you actually accomplish anything or not!*

And no, I'm not suggesting you create a smokescreen of "busy-work" to masquerade as productivity. I'm saying there are specific actions you can take to bring positive attention to yourself, which can produce definite advantages to your career.

Here are seven suggestions I've personally used that will get you noticed:

• Periodically solicit customer feedback on some specific function of your service or product. For example: Do customers like the idea of overnight delivery, or is the additional cost too high? How does the quality of your product or service compare to the competition? How can customer service be improved? Circulate the results to the appropriate department heads *after* sharing them with your boss.

• Obtain testimonials from your customers (and from their customers if your company sells wholesale) about the quality and availability of your product or service. Ask for details about an unusual application or how a customer solved a particularly difficult or serious problem using your product or service. If possible, use video to document the experience, and make sure you're in it. Show it to your supervisor, then mutually determine a list of product managers, marketing heads, and customers who should receive a copy.

- Send regular internal correspondence to employees in other divisions and company locations who influenced some aspect of a sale, resolved a customer complaint, or created a positive experience for you, your subordinate, or customer. Thank them for their contribution and make sure to copy your supervisor in the letter or email.

- Write a regular (monthly, bi-monthly, or weekly) newsletter. Send it to your customers with updates on products, services, applications, problem-solving suggestions, tips on improving communications, and other information relevant within your industry. Distribute by email using a free mailing service like Mail Chimp (free up to 2000 pieces per month, as of this writing).

- Present an in-house seminar or training class for customers or staff. I've mentioned this elsewhere in the book because it's one of the most powerful actions you can take to bring attention to yourself as a leader. Don't expect any additional compensation, but most supervisors will allow you to use company time for preparation and delivery if you can show how the content of the program will translate into increased sales, greater productivity, a more positive work environment, or a reduction of company liability.

- Create an industry blog featuring your products, services, and applications. Invite customers, employees, your supervisor, and industry influencers to write guest posts. To be effective, you'll need to post something new at least once a week. Make sure your boss understands that you do this during your off-hours to alleviate any concerns over subordinating your core job responsibilities to the blog.

- Tell your supervisor you'd like to volunteer to help with office new hires. When explaining the specific ways in which you can contribute, offer to be the first point of contact to answer questions, resolve a problem, or obtain advice. Your intention is to take some of the load off the supervisor. Confirm that your regular work responsibilities limit your availability, but you also understand the need to bring new hires up to speed as quickly as possible, and you'll make the time when it's needed.

These are just some of the ways to let your boss know you're focused on your career and invested in your work. Your specific assignment will no doubt produce additional opportunities unique to your job function. Always start with the ones easiest to implement. You'll be surprised how small but consistent efforts are interpreted by management as indications of your commitment to the company.

ROGER A. REID

Chapter Eighteen
Your Age—Does it Matter?

I've heard this subject debated back and forth in Job-Fair seminars, with HR types quoting anti-discrimination law to a front-row full of sixty-year-olds who sit there shaking their heads as they hold up resumes they've been sending out continuously for eight months.

Unfortunately, the subject is plagued with inaccurate generalities, such as:

• The older employee is inflexible, slow to respond, and not able to keep up with their younger counterparts. Their most productive years are behind them, and they're just coasting to retirement.

• Younger employees are not ready to commit to a career and have placed *their* priorities ahead of the company's. They can be brash, impulsive, require immediate gratification, and usually make poor decisions in the long-term.

Some of these beliefs are so permeated within the current work culture, that "pre-emptive warnings" are commonplace. I've even heard management consultants advise a room full of Millennials to take on extra responsibility and show up early and stay late to counteract the widely held misconception that the younger generation puts far more emphasis on their personal life than their career.

The truth?

Attitudes toward younger hires and aging employees vary with the particular company. A good barometer is often reflected by the average age of a company employee. While the number may not necessarily reflect the company's predisposition about the preferred age of their workforce, it *can* tell you a lot about how you'll fit in.

For example, if you're fifty-five and applying for a job at a software development firm where the average age is under thirty, you're going to stand out like a sore thumb. More than the possibility of feeling uncomfortable with the age gap, you may also experience difficulty in having your ideas and opinions considered with equal weight to that of someone half your age.

Is that fair?

We're not talking about fair. We're talking about cultural and environmental influences reflected in the workplace, and occasionally, within an entire industry.

In general, the larger the company, the more you'll find age diversity, simply because a greater number of employees is more likely to reflect the demographics of the general adult population. For example, in a larger company, an annual flock of new hires, typically right out of school, will join an established and aging workforce, resulting in a more "age-balanced" environment.

However, there are exceptions. Typically referred to as "new generation" industries, these high-tech startups often internally clone themselves as an (erroneous?) prerequisite of ensuring technical and market familiarity. This preference for younger employees assumes older workers are not as likely to possess the specific education, training, or be aware of the rapidly changing competitive influences associated with the products and services these companies produce.

Before we continue, it's important to understand that age bias and prejudice can happen at both ends of the spectrum. While most people associate age discrimination with the aging employee—someone who is destined to be managed out and replaced with a younger counterpart, or an older worker who is passed over for a promotion in favor of someone younger—the reverse situation can also be true.

Here's an example of age-mature preference: I'd been with Acme about six months when the VP of sales invited the current crop of new-hires to lunch. We'd assembled in Milwaukee for a week of training, and the lunch invitation was a customary tradition to increase rapport between management and the company's newbies.

On the day of the luncheon, we were told we would not be eating in any ordinary restaurant, but were about to have a rare and unusual experience. The company had reserved the dining room at a private club that catered specifically to elderly men . . . *and their fathers.*

Acme's upper-level management received membership in this age-honoring establishment as a perk, an indication that a preferred criterion to move up into the lofty levels of management was a birthday at least fifty years in the past. Like a fine cheese, you were expected to age a bit before you were considered worthy of joining the big table.

Isn't age bias against the law? Yes, outright age discrimination is illegal, so it's doubtful you'll be confronted with overt prejudice due to your age. However, you *will* be judged, labeled, sorted, and ranked due to age-related issues— *including your appearance.*

Your best defense against age discrimination? Use the following suggestions to mitigate management's tendency to categorize an employee's potential based on age, regardless of which end of the age scale is the prevailing norm demonstrated by your industry or company bias.

• **Your appearance.** First, avoid trendy or untraditional styles in your choice of clothing. Get rid of the nose and lip piercings. Unless you're working in an industry where idiosyncratic self-expression is a celebrated part of the work-place, your appearance should reflect the same style-values you see conveyed by your supervisor. If you choose to ignore the obvious norms of your work environment, management will interpret this as putting your own needs before the company's—and that makes you expendable. For example, wild hair colors and styles are fine for club dates and private parties. But if you want to be considered for fast-track advancement, get a conservative, flattering haircut and keep it maintained. Showing up with a pink-tipped Mohawk may be an expression of the real you, but it could also resign you to a basic work assignment without a real future.

- **Send a subliminal signal that you're ready to move up** *now.* A few years ago, Harvard Business Review featured an article that claimed the average age of a corporate employee promoted to their first management position is thirty. This is a bit younger than the generally *perceived* age of a first-time manager (thirty-five), but I think it's safe to say that initial management opportunities tend to be available to those in the thirty to thirty-five-year age range.

If you're twenty-six, does that mean you can wait four years before worrying about presenting a professional appearance? In a word, no. Especially if you expect to find that coveted management opportunity waiting for you.

If you need an example of your company's expectations, look at your current manager. That's your model. If your manager is of the opposite sex, look for a same-sex management counterpart. If she wears a suit or slacks with a jacket, and you work in the same environment, do the same.

You can also take a cue from the most successful in your job category. As a sales engineer working out of the Phoenix office, I quickly adopted the accepted uniform of the day: a pair of slacks and a conservative, button-down shirt. It was a comfortable change from the Denver office, where I wore a suit and tie every day. However, during a training junket to Los Angeles, I saw the LA salespeople adhered to the same dress code I'd seen in Denver. So did those from San Francisco, Salt Lake City, Seattle, and Portland.

Phoenix was the exception. The city's laid-back, informal atmosphere influenced the fashion of business, and while there was no appreciable difference in sales performance between Phoenix and the other offices, over the next few years, I noticed the employees from other locations getting the lion's share of the promotions. Looking back, I can see how "looking the part" influenced upper management's decisions. Those suit-wearing salespeople were dressing like managers, a subtle signal they were ready to step up and perform the function more effectively than someone who didn't appear interested in the position because of the way they dressed.

- **Be "proactively appropriate"—regardless of your age.** Just because you're twenty-two doesn't give you an excuse to be silly or irresponsible. And turning sixty doesn't give you license to skip out on meetings or grant yourself invented privileges because you've celebrated your thirtieth anniversary with the company. If the office setting is a serious, strictly business environment, don't make yourself conspicuous by being the boisterous exception. You may receive a few nods from your co-workers to acknowledge your moxie, but you could also lose favor with the boss. Conversely, if the atmosphere is informal or even playful, and your work personality is more introverted, make sure your less-expressive behavior is not interpreted as judgmental or as being critical of your co-workers. You'll need their support and even their endorsement, especially when you receive an opportunity for advancement.

- **Demonstrate your proficiency.** Keep in mind that job descriptions are written to define the minimum expectations for the position. Doing the minimum will get you by—for a while. But sooner or later, management will want to see you demonstrate the talent and motivation required to move up and handle more responsibility—*even if you remain in the same position for your entire career.* And that's true regardless of your age. Always give the impression that you're not only good at your work, you also excel at it. It's difficult to use someone's age against them when they're doing an outstanding job. If you're concerned about your competency, work on the specific issues that need improvement.

For example, if you don't feel confident about your ability to make customer presentations, find someone who does and watch them in action. Determine which repeated behaviors you want to emulate, then adapt them to your own style. If you have trouble with reports or other types of paperwork, ask if you can see a well-written example. In most cases, you can copy format, style, layout, and design, with the resulting improvements enhancing management's perception of your work. In a corporate environment, this is rarely considered plagiarism and is often interpreted as making an effort to get it right.

- **"Popularize" your personality.** Give yourself a "personality check." How do people react when you speak? Is your voice too loud? Do you dominate the conversation and rarely give others a chance to talk? Do you show interest in what others are saying, or just wait for the opportunity to interrupt? The old 80/20 rule is an excellent standard to measure the correct ratio of listening to talking. And yes, it still means letting others talk eighty percent of the time. By keeping your input to about twenty percent of the conversation and showing interest when others are speaking, you'll be demonstrating an essential trait of people who are considered charismatic and admired. Those adhering to this formula are popular because of how they make others feel, not necessarily because of what they personally contribute to a conversation.

Chapter Nineteen
Feeling Stuck, Stifled, and Stagnant

The infrequent high points of a corporate career—receiving a bonus, a performance award, or a promotion—seldom offset the day-to-day repetition of your daily work. The endless reports, team meetings, and countless hours on the phone can, over time, become monotonous and boring.

Yes, you're compensated for doing it, but when you can't see the personal value in it, when the work no longer motivates or provides a sense of purpose, you're breaking rocks and moving sand piles. No matter how exciting, rewarding, or gratifying your job initially seemed, there will be times when you wonder if this is the way you want to spend the rest of your working life.

Feeling unappreciated or trapped in a work situation that's unfulfilling or falls short of your expectations are ailments often associated with working for someone else. Media hype typically takes it a step further, suggesting these kinds of complaints are exclusive to those working under the corporate umbrella, and that it comes with the territory. However, don't make the mistake of believing the symptoms of predictable repetition are experienced only by employees. In reality, they're typical complaints expressed by *all* workers—regardless of who steers the ship.

The specific cause or reason varies from person to person. Maybe it's going to the same place every day, doing the same thing for months, years, or even decades. Sometimes, it's the result of constantly seeing the same people, or realizing the next fifty meetings won't make a difference in the way *you* feel about your life.

Part of the problem is what psychologists call *habituation,* a term describing the progressive loss of the initial sense of satisfaction or pleasure we feel when doing something for the first time. (This is a close cousin to *hedonic adaptation,* which describes the tendency for humans to return to a pre-established happiness set-point, regardless of the unfolding life events and circumstances.) If the amount of satisfaction and pleasure continues to decrease, personal gratification will eventually fall below the individual's threshold of value—especially when it's measured as the loss of opportunity to be doing something else.

Here's a typical example. An account executive easily recalls the raw exhilaration of success when her boss congratulated her on landing that first large account. Then she brought in her second big account, and while it still felt good, it didn't deliver the same stratospheric high she'd felt immediately following her first success. By the time she booked her tenth client, it had become business as usual—bringing in new clients was the norm, and anything less was unacceptable.

That's the way it is with any repeated activity. Even those engaging in high-risk and high-sensory professions—for example, skydivers, race car drivers, and test pilots—readily admit the adrenaline rush accompanying their first-time experience isn't the same after they've repeated the process a hundred times. At that point, many aspects of the activity, including the ones responsible for their first euphoric high, have become routine, or even a bit tedious. This is especially true when the activity becomes normalized with the need to make improvements, evaluate procedures, and elevate performance to the next level.

Another good example comes from those in the entertainment business. In an industry where movie stars, singers, musicians, and stage entertainers are surrounded by glamor and glitz, it's difficult to imagine their work as tedious or repetitive. But when they're away from the pageantry and spectacle, these high-achievers talk about the intensity of rehearsals, the endless hours of study and practice, and the need for constant discipline to meet the expectations of a demanding audience. Even in the spotlight, with thousands of admirers watching their every move, it's become a job.

Here's the big question: Does a lack of motivation mean it's time to move on? It depends. Have you outgrown your job? Or are you feeling the effects of a disappointing week or an unwanted or unpleasant change in policy? Rather than a change in employers, you may simply need a break—a chance to look at the bigger picture and view the situation with perspective.

Rx for boredom at work: Take a vacation. Afraid to take a *real* vacation? Concerned your absence will hurt your career? A large percentage of management-level employees—especially Loyalists—believe they shouldn't take more than a few days off at a time. While they may think their sacrifice is good for the company and beneficial to their career, the truth is just the opposite.

Studies show those who believe they've become indispensable—and therefore refuse to take an extended vacation—are the employees most likely to develop stress-related illnesses and problems with alcohol and drugs. They're also the most likely to leave a promising career that is temporarily stalled because their perspective is compromised.

Enlightened managers know the importance of vacations. Realizing the positive, long-term mental and physical health benefits that result from taking time away from the office, they often insist their subordinates take vacations that are at least a week in duration. So before making any kind of career decision based on a lack of motivation or loss of enthusiasm for the job, take a break. Stay available by phone, text, or email if you have to, but set aside at least eight to ten hours a day with the cell phone and computer turned *off.* Just being in a different environment for a week can do wonders for your attitude.

What if a vacation doesn't bring relief? If your return to work immediately buries you beneath the same dark, suffocating cloud you were under before you left, it's time to take a hard look at what's going on—with you *and* your employer.

Start by making a list of the tasks and related job functions you absolutely hate. Then determine how much of your time is dedicated to these tasks. If it's twenty percent or less, you've got a situation that can be managed or changed. If it's fifty percent or more, you're in the wrong job.

Let's look at the positive side first. If eighty percent of your job activities are enjoyable, acceptable, or at least tolerable, determine if the unacceptable twenty percent can be delegated or outsourced. This may require talking with your manager about your need to increase your effectiveness, and what this would mean to the company in terms of added productivity.

Another option is to covertly train a co-worker to handle the work. In return, you offer to help with an equivalent measure of their work or compensate them for their time. If you go this route, *never reveal this arrangement to anyone.* Management generally prohibits the unofficial outsourcing of any job-related responsibility to another employee. However, despite this restriction, I've known plenty of salespeople and mid-level managers who personally compensated their co-workers for handling paperwork, reports, phone calls, and other time-intensive tasks. The resulting refocus of their energy allowed them to concentrate on more productive activities.

What if your list of disagreeable activities takes up fifty percent (or more) of your schedule? It's time to face reality: You need a different job. And while that means you'll need to change your activities and responsibilities, it's not always necessary to change employers. Before looking elsewhere for a new position, make sure you've exhausted every possible opportunity for a job change or transfer within your current company. By taking advantage of an internal transfer to a more suitable job assignment, you'll retain your employment history and seniority–an important factor when being considered for advancement and promotion.

A new job search within your current company should be based on a comprehensive and organized plan of action—no less intensive than if you were approaching a new company for the first time.

Applying for a position from inside versus outside your company can provide a real advantage. However, the key is to make sure your request results in *job equilibrium* for the company.

When it comes to staffing and reassignment, management works on the status quo of equilibrium. Filling one hole by creating another doesn't solve their problem. It just shifts it, creating a new vacancy that still has to be filled. And this is the important part: *Moving an employee from a position in which he or she is productive is inherently risky*. If the transferred employee doesn't work out in the new position, management now has two vacancies to fill.

But doesn't an existing employee have a default advantage over an unproven jobseeker? While it's true that a transferred worker is already familiar with company policy and directives, familiarity with company procedures and programs is not considered to be such an overwhelming advantage—on singular merit—to move their name to the top of the list for consideration.

So if you work in accounting, and want to transfer to marketing, or fleet management, or R & D, you'll need to build a strong case for yourself—one that will convince management the move will benefit the company in the long-term.

Letting management know of your desire to move can be tricky (and downright risky). Unless your manager mentions a vacancy in conversation or you're personally presented with the opportunity, avoid making a general statement of wanting to be considered for work in other divisions or locations. It's an indication of your dissatisfaction with your current situation. In short, you're saying you're unhappy and want a change. Even a reasonable boss can interpret your request for a transfer as an indication you're not one hundred percent committed to your current job. They'll assume your mind is elsewhere and you're in the process of looking for something better—which could also include a position at another company. In short, they may consider you *half-gone*, and they're not going to give you their attention and priority if you're making plans to leave your current position.

The worst-case reaction? It usually comes from a short-sighted supervisor who sees little difference between someone who wants a change and the constant complainer who doesn't like his job and his productivity is suffering because of it. Ego-maniacal bosses are easily offended and will make sure you get the change you're looking for—right out the door.

The key is in your approach—how you present the idea of a transfer. Stay under the radar by staying "passively" aware. That means waiting until you hear about a new opening that interests you. If you have a friend who is in the company's HR pipeline, *and you trust them to keep their mouth shut*, ask them for a head's up if they hear of an opening in an area or division that interests you. When it happens, it's time to speak up. Timing is everything. Your request must be originated between the time the vacancy occurs and before the company fills it.

Here's a suggested method of bringing it up to your boss:

"I heard about the opening in the San Diego office. If you don't have someone in mind, I'd like to be considered. My wife has always wanted to live there because it would put her closer to her family. Personally, I'm happy here, but I promised my wife I'd ask, and of course, there could be a real opportunity there."

Notice that the primary reason for the move has nothing to do with YOU. Always make sure your request for a change is to accommodate a family member or is motivated by an influence outside of your current job or working conditions. This might include such things as health (not yours), educational opportunities for your kids (a specialized curriculum or internship at the new location), or a move to a warmer or dryer climate.

Then, leave it alone. Don't bring it up again. If management decides you're the right person for the job, they'll let you know. However, if you're told the position was filled from the outside or from another office, reply in the positive: "Good. I'm sure that will work out best for everyone. Thanks for letting me know."

Never show any disappointment. And don't ask why you didn't receive the consideration you were hoping for. Your boss may have blocked your request. Or she may have other plans for you down the road. Accept the decision gracefully (because you're not going to change it with a hissy-fit), and assure your immediate superior that it was the right decision.

If you've exhausted your search for other possible job opportunities within your current company and believe you're "locked-in" without the possibility of a transfer, it's time to look elsewhere.

As I've stressed before, keep your job search a secret from everyone! Do your best to covey a positive attitude about your current position and continue to do solid, responsible work. Your goal is to maintain your current income for as long as possible—until you've accepted an offer from another employer.

Chapter Twenty
Signs It's Time to Leave

Don't ignore the warning signs! There are several warning signals that indicate your relationship with your employer is in jeopardy. Some are financial or objectively based and have to do with the (failing) internal operation of the company. Others involve the absence of future job opportunities (assuming you want to move up), management's assessment of your current and future value, and your compensation, in comparison to others who are performing at the same level of productivity.

Here are five of the most frequent symptoms of a failing employer-employee relationship:

You're working for a small company that's losing money. Financial liquidity is a necessity for any size organization, but it's especially vital for a smaller company, especially one with low cash reserves or that lacks the credit line of a Fortune 500.

Restrictions on expenses, cut-backs on company perks and benefits, and termination of high-salaried "wonder boys," are all indications of a company in trouble. Waiting around for the company to go out of business will only decrease your leverage in finding a new position because then, you'll *need* a job instead of being able to negotiate from the stronger position of being employed but willing to change for the right offer. I've mentioned this before, but the adage is still true: You're most hirable when you're already employed.

You've topped out. Maybe it's politics, or there's no room at the next logical level for promotion, but whatever the reason, there's no clear path for advancement. If moving up is your goal, you'll need to look elsewhere for new opportunities.

You don't get along with your boss. I'm not talking about the occasional disagreement over a procedure or a decision you didn't like. I'm referring to a total impasse, where you feel blocked at every turn, or when it's impossible to have a productive conversation or a simple exchange of ideas. You're always on guard, and you're sure your manager is ready to hang you out to dry. Don't try to fight the situation, outmaneuver it, or outlast it. You're wasting your time. On the outside chance that senior management knows your boss is a problem, and given the choice, would rather keep you and let her go, they'll let you know *after* you submit your resignation. If you don't hear from them, consider their silence a clear confirmation you made the right decision.

You don't like the work. Maybe you enjoy working with computers and writing code. You've built websites for your friends and spent hours designing simple apps for your own use. Receiving a job offer from a major software company seemed like a Godsend. However, five years later, you're stuck in testing and debugging. You've asked for a transfer and made it clear you want to do original design work, but the company needs you right where you are because you're good at your job and they're up to their eyeballs in applications from people who want to work in design. They value your current contribution, and they see no benefit in making a change. You've essentially become the proverbial square peg force-fitted into a round hole, and the company is happy to keep you there.

Here's the big question: How much longer—how many more years of your life—do you want to spend working in testing and debugging? If you don't feel comfortable putting a deadline on your career path, ask yourself this: If you feel any hesitancy in sending out your resume, how will you feel about the situation in another five years—if nothing changes?

Before you jump ship, keep in mind that *all* work, repeated over and over, can become tedious. More important, what originally excited you about your job may have changed because the industry has changed. Make sure your job dissatisfaction isn't the result of a nostalgic pull from the good old days. Future success in your career will be difficult to achieve if it's fueled by unrealistic expectations from the past.

Your company is being taken over by a larger firm. Although we covered this topic in detail in another chapter, it's difficult to overestimate the negative impact a buyout or takeover can have on your career. When a larger company acquires a smaller one, it isn't long before the new parent company begins to flex its muscles. Consider a buyout, takeover, or reorganization a wake-up call—a signal to take a hard look at your career and evaluate your options. Review your contingency plan and update your list of possible new job prospects. You may even want to consider putting out a few "feelers" to test the market. You'd be surprised at the number of employees that ignore the obvious signs and believe their job is secure, despite the foundational changes taking place all around them.

Chapter Twenty-One
Harassment in the Workplace

Although this is one of the shortest chapters in the book, for some readers, it may be the most important. The suggestions that follow can be used for any situation in which you believe your right to earn a livelihood in a non-threatening, safe environment is being compromised or outright violated.

Before initiating a formal complaint, arm yourself with an understanding of the law and your options for legal recourse. Consult with an employment attorney to obtain a clear understanding of where you can reasonably draw the line and expect your employer to respect those boundaries.

Knowing this in advance will give you a sense of confidence in negotiating a reasonable solution—whether you stay with your employer or decide to leave.

Harassment comes in two general forms:

1. Discrimination, in which an employee is subjected to verbal comments or physical actions predicated on their religion, race, sex, age, sexual orientation, or other protected class. Harassment can include unwanted physical contact, sexual innuendo, coercion, threats, or intimidation.

2. A deliberate campaign waged by management to motivate an employee to quit, or the gathering of "evidence" to substantiate termination. In this situation, the goal is to remove the employee while mitigating the liability of a wrongful termination lawsuit. This is often referred to as being "managed out."

In a previous chapter, I talked about the possibility of being the target of harassment or some form of discrimination. From the standpoint of keeping your job, I stated that making a legal claim of any kind against the company usually brings the kiss of death to your career. And that's true, *regardless of your rights as defined by law.*

Obviously, a large part of deciding what to do and when to do it is based on the severity of the infraction. If the negative event(s) has robbed you of any desire to stay a single day longer with your current employer, then your options are clear. However, if you want to preserve the relationship, try approaching the source of the problem privately with your supervisor. Start by saying how much you like your job, and you want to clear up a situation that's bothering you. Explain your position, how the behavior makes you feel, and ask for the behavior or situation to be changed or eliminated. End the conversation by expressing your appreciation for her consideration and your promise that your conversation will remain private.

Here's a suggested order of actions to handle a personal grievance:

1. Document each time the event happens. Write down the date, the time, the names of the individuals involved, and include any witnesses and a description of what happened. Keep this in a notebook AT HOME. Never leave any derogatory or damaging evidence at the office, and never reveal to anyone that you have it.

2. Document any actions, communications, or face-to-face meetings you have to resolve the issue, regardless of whether it's with a co-worker or supervisor. Include the details of how long the meeting or conversation lasted, what was discussed, and what was decided, proposed, or resolved.

3. Run your situation by an attorney. This creates a third-party confirmation of the problem *at the time it takes place.* Establishing a verifiable, contemporaneous record of the situation and its impact on you—can be an effective tool if you need to take legal action. This may also be important in meeting

any statute of limitations when filing a formal complaint or lawsuit.

I want to stress that these situations can be complicated and may originate from an intentional plan to terminate, or the personal agenda of a superior—motivations that you're unaware of. Just keep in mind there's a time to try to negotiate and a time to lower the boom on prejudice and extortion. Discuss your options with someone you trust—your spouse, a close friend who can keep their mouth shut, or a family member with a comparable professional background to yours. Factor in the advice from an attorney, and then decide the best way of dealing with the problem.

I'll move on from this rather ugly topic with this: Being able to settle, manage, or otherwise successfully negotiate problems is what management expects from their best and brightest. From the company's mindset, airing their dirty laundry in public is de-facto proof you're not senior management material. Conversely, there's going to be a few bad apples in every workplace, and if push comes to shove, it may be your place to confront them, and if necessary, take legal action against the organization to stop the abusive behavior. If you feel conflicted about which road to take, ask yourself how you'll feel about yourself and your situation six months from now—if you do nothing. The difference between compromise and sacrifice may be difficult to recognize during the heat of conflict, but your outcome will generally be more satisfying in the long term if you consider your self-respect among your most valuable—and non-negotiable—assets.

Chapter Twenty-Two
Exit Strategies

You've made the decision . . . It's time to leave!

Perhaps you've realized you've gone as far as you can go with your current employer and a promotion to the next level is only available from another company. Or maybe you're tired of the type of work you're doing, or you've learned that your division will soon be re-organized and downsized. Whatever the reason, your focus is now on the future—with a different employer.

Remember, there's a real sense of liberation in leaving a job when you know it's the right decision. Once you've made a personal commitment to move on, it's simply a matter of making your transition as financially stable as possible.

If the company wants to keep you, expect a bit of psychological warfare. Informing your boss that you're planning to leave the company—especially after you've been there for several years—can cue the violins. If they want to keep you, they may even respond with a touch of resentment, confronting your motives and bringing your loyalty into question. Don't be surprised if they get down and dirty about it, suggesting how leaving could affect not only your professional standing but your personal reputation as well. Regardless of their approach, ignore it. It's a ploy, an attempt to guilt you into staying.

Should loyalty influence your decision? From the company's perspective, loyalty isn't a measurable metric. Yes, the company enjoys the benefits of employee loyalty from the added leverage it brings to *their* side of salary negotiations and employee retention, but rarely is a company motivated to treat you with greater consideration because of *your* loyalty.

Companies determine an employee's value based on the impact they have on productivity, profit, market share, or other objective and measurable metrics—*in comparison to how much they pay for it.* That's all there is to it. Your value to your employer is based on that simple equation. Showing up early for twenty years and leaving your desk clean at the end of every workday won't buy you an extra day's severance when the layoffs begin.

Any consideration you choose to place on loyalty—I'm talking about that generic, un-qualified, un-measurable, warm-fuzzy emotional component—is a show of weakness. Never let it creep into your evaluation of a counter-offer from your current employer. You'll lose your negotiating edge. In the worst case, you'll make the wrong decision.

Be prepared to handle "Pre-exit Remorse." Giving up a sure thing in exchange for the unknown can fill you with anxiety and doubt. You may find yourself asking, "Am I doing the right thing? Will I regret my decision in a few months?"

These questions stem from a natural defense mechanism left over from our ancestors who wrestled with the decision to stay inside the cave (where it was safe) or venture outside and face the unknown risks of a hostile environment. And just as our forefathers realized the benefits of leaving the cave—fresh meat, establishing trade with other tribes, enhanced social interaction—far outweighed the risks, the advantages of moving from a stagnate career to one with plenty of headroom for growth can be life-changing.

Here's the good news: The majority of our pre-change anxiety results from an imagined worst-case scenario—which is usually a far less accurate prediction of the future than the actual outcome. If giving up the familiar in exchange for the unknown is a huge challenge for you, think of it in the same way you would if you were breaking up with a girlfriend or boyfriend.

The level of stress and discomfort peaks right after the breakup—and that's when most people begin second-guessing their decision.

What if I never find someone as nice, smart, sexy, understanding, or attractive as she was? Should I have stayed with him? I wonder if it's too late to talk her into taking me back?

Those questions continue to haunt you every lonely minute until you have your first date with someone new. And then, sometime between the second glass of wine and dessert, you realize how short-sighted you've been. As time passes and your new relationship continues to grow, you'll seldom think about old what's-her-name, and when you do, you'll be thankful you decided to end that relationship and move on to someone better suited for you.

Here are two bottom-line considerations to keep in mind if you find yourself caught between the comfort and familiarity of your current job and the temptation of a better offer from a competitor:

- **Moving from one company to another is often the only way to raise your total compensation.** The fastest way to move up into the ranks of management is usually by strategic transfers to other companies. If and when another company approaches you, give their offer plenty of consideration before deciding. Your perceived value to the competition is high because of the promise of immediate gain in the form of your existing relationships with customers, vendors, and influencers. A competitor will also pay you for your experience, technical know-how, communication skills, and emotional maturity— much of which was developed under the guidance and coaching of your past employer.

- **The company *always* does what's best for the company.** Period. End of story. Most job functions are under constant scrutiny to determine if there is a more effective and less expensive way to accomplish it. No job is safe from outsourcing. Your only defense is to be constantly aware of other opportunities, *making sure your first loyalty is always to yourself.* You're especially vulnerable if your work falls into an area identified as most likely to be replaced by a third-party source. For example, accounting, training, fleet management, IT (including web presence and inter-company computer systems and security), physical plant security, customer service, legal services, and in fact, just about anything that doesn't require face-to-face time with customers. And that's only because many companies are reluctant to give up control of how the company's image is presented and ultimately perceived by customers. However, even customer imprinting and its effect on sales are often reduced to a question of profit. There's an entire industry dedicated to the independent representation of company sales and service, with contract sales reps typically handling multiple, non-competing product lines within a common industry.

Never believe you or your job position is immune to the effects of restructuring, downsizing, or layoffs. If your compensation is significantly more than what a younger, less experienced replacement would cost, you're vulnerable.

What if changing employers ends up being a mistake? It happens. Maybe the congenial, easy-going manager you met during the interview process turns out to be an ego-maniacal, narcissistic lunatic. Or the managerial position you were promised never materializes, or is filled with another candidate because "you're doing such a good job where you are."

The most common complaints from those wishing they could manifest a "do-over" are usually based on a misrepresentation or a misunderstanding about the new job responsibilities, the company's unforeseen negative political climate, or an unexpected and severe decline in the company's financial strength. Regardless of the reason, if you find yourself in this situation, you have a problem.

Leaving too soon—within a couple of months or even within a year of being hired—can result in being labeled a *job-hopper,* someone who is unreliable and unpredictable, characteristics not generally associated with candidates for a mid-level or senior management position.

With rare exceptions, a quick exit is going to be difficult to rationalize to your *next* employer. They'll want to know what happened. Saying you left to distance yourself from a hostile atmosphere or a boss who made unreasonable demands may sound justified, but remember, unless the interviewer knows you personally or is intimately familiar with your previous situation, there's going to be some underlying suspicion that *you couldn't handle it.* And that's a reflection on *you.*

Even with a reasonable, logical explanation exonerating you from blame, it's nearly impossible to completely neutralize the uncertainty of your motives. Worse case fallout? A new employer will wonder if you'll do the same thing—quit—the moment you're faced with a difficult challenge.

So how long do you have to stick it out before you can confidently move to another company? Opinions vary based on the industry, but the unofficial consensus among corporate managers is a minimum of one year. Leaving in less than a year will raise immediate questions about your intentions and character.

Does that mean you have to serve a minimum sentence of one year to avoid acquiring the stigma of a "quitter?" If you're going to stay in the same industry and successfully move to another company without a lot of baggage, *that's exactly what it means.*

If you find yourself in this situation—a short-timer who hates his job—try to find ways to insulate yourself from negative people and situations while finding methods to make a meaningful contribution to the company's productivity. Sitting back and waiting for the time to pass is inviting dismissal. Being terminated for cause within the first year will leave a black mark on your career that's nearly impossible to erase.

The best way to mitigate the risk of moving to a new employer? Avoid being emotionally swayed by false bravado. A job offer from the competition can be intoxicating. Your ego is on a joy-ride because another company is willing to pay a premium for your talent, experience, and ability.

Here's the trap: We tend to assume we know all we need to know about our new future employer, because, hell, *they want us.* And that *has* to go a long way in revealing the kind of people they are, as well as how we can expect to be treated. It's an emotionally driven assumption that can easily lead to a false sense of obligation: *It's almost as if we have to say "yes."*

Turning down their offer would be tantamount to an insult. And we certainly don't want to insult someone who is complimenting us with an offer of employment.

If you find yourself having these kinds of thoughts, STOP. Accepting an offer out of emotionally-charged enthusiasm is the best way to regret your decision later. Make sure you're making an informed choice and not letting your ego push you into a job that isn't right.

Treat any new job offer as if it's your first. Perform due diligence by doing the research described in an earlier chapter. After subjecting the company to a rigorous examination, if you still feel positive about committing the next several years to them, you can move forward, knowing you made best efforts to uncover any hidden skeletons that could haunt your future success.

What if your research turns up some concerns? Before bringing these up to your potential new boss, decide how important they are. Eliminate the non-critical and minor points and focus only on the deal-breakers. Then make a personal commitment to either accept or decline the offer based on having your concerns resolved to your satisfaction. In other words, your decision is contingent upon receiving answers that resolve the problem(s). If, after additional discussion or correspondence, you still have red flags, your answer should be a career-saving "no."

Is there ever a time to "listen" to your emotions and feelings? If, after receiving a reasonable explanation that objectively dispels your concerns, *and you're still hesitant or can't decide for some inexplicable reason*, then turn the offer down. There's something else going on, and your subconscious is trying to tell you the job isn't right for you.

Here's a personal example of letting personal feelings and emotions influence the decision process: I'd worked for Acme for about seven years when a manager from ITE approached me about a branch manager's position in Tucson. ITE was a highly respected manufacturer of electrical distribution equipment and quite often, an Acme competitor on large projects. I was curious, so I agreed to meet with the local manager. After an initial half-hour conversation, a lunch appointment was scheduled with the regional manager. A week later, I was listening to Mr. Regional recite a list of benefits I would enjoy as an employee of ITE. Before I could finish my salad, he offered me the job—including a large raise in pay—right after he ordered a second scotch and water.

At the time, I was relatively young—thirty. And I was comfortable at Acme. I liked the work, the customers, and my co-workers.

And the money? It sucked. But my real estate investments generated an income that far exceeded my annual salary from Acme, so my compensation, at least from a big-picture perspective, was not my primary concern.

I thanked the ITE manager for the offer and told him I needed time to think about it.

Here's what was going through my mind: The ITE Corporation manufactured quality equipment and had an excellent reputation within the industry. And while they could be very competitive in a bidding situation, their product line was limited to electrical distribution equipment.

Acme, my current employer, not only manufactured distribution products, but industrial controls and systems. Many third-party architects and engineers often specified the Acme brand as "No Equal" (meaning a competitive brand could not be used). I was employed by a recognized leader in the industry, granting me a level of status acknowledged by both customers and the competition. In short, Acme sales-engineers were considered to be some of the best in the business.

At the time, that was important to me. Leaving Acme would change *my* branding. I couldn't help but think I was taking a step backward.

I shared my situation with a long-time Acme employee. He'd seen plenty of managers come and go, and if anyone could give me an objective opinion, I was sure it was him.

"Take the ITE job," he said. "In ten years, you'll be a regional manager. Maybe higher. ITE has always had the reputation of rewarding talented people who want to advance.

"But what about my job here at Acme?" I asked.

"Acme is an old, conservative company that loves the status quo. Right now, they see you as a productive employee. Your customers like you, you're self-motivated, and you generate plenty of profitable business. You'd think those attributes would be reasons to promote you. But that's not the way Acme's management thinks. As long as you're doing a good job, they have no reason to move you up. In fact, there's a good chance they'll keep you in the field as a sales engineer until you're ready to retire."

"So you're telling me Acme hires managers primarily from the outside?" I asked.

"Not always. But the people who receive promotions are usually the ones who were just average sales engineers and customer reps. They typically struggled with day-to-day customer problems, put policy before people, and couldn't make a decision without running every little detail past their boss."

"That doesn't sound like someone qualified to be a good manager," I said.

"It's all in how you define it. The Acme regional guys want their subordinate managers to toe the line, to fit the traditional profile. They want someone who thinks the only way to solve a problem is to write a report, set up a meeting, and then have a three-martini lunch."

"So if I want a promotion from Acme, I need to back off on the time I'm devoting to sales and spend more time on paperwork and internal BS?"

He nodded. "In my opinion, if you stay at Acme and keep performing at 150 percent of quota, it's doubtful you'll ever advance beyond your current position."

It sounded like good advice. In fact, it sounded like the truth.

But it wasn't my truth. I believed that in another year or two, I would be given an opportunity to advance into management. My boss had already talked to me about the projected growth of the Phoenix office and the eventual need for a branch manager. He added that I was the most likely candidate for the job.

Looking back, staying with Acme was a critical career mistake. I allowed a sense of loyalty and the vague promise of a better future to taint my decision. In hindsight, I realize my wiser co-worker was correct about the management styles of both Acme and ITE—a fact I should have extrapolated from researching the career paths of managers from both companies.

So do your homework. Don't allow your emotions to get the better of you. Make a decision that will result in the best choice for *you*, based on the empirical clues left by other employees who currently hold the job you ultimately want to fill.

What if your goal is to leave your industry entirely? Let's say you're sick of marketing computers, or selling agricultural equipment, or you never want to hear about the cosmetics business again for as long as you live. Even if you're sure your skills and experience are easily transferable, you'll need to do plenty of research before you can determine if a new industry is going to be a good fit.

Customer mindset and buying criteria are often industry-specific, especially if you're moving from an industrial market to one that is consumer-based, or vice-versa. The process of marketing can also be vastly different.

Ask yourself how comfortable you'll be in an environment that is radically different from the one you're familiar with? What about compensation? Is it equivalent to your current job? How many companies are major players? Where are they located? What's the potential to move up? What's the typical career path of a mid-level manager? You're looking for positive signs that indicate a reasonable probability of making a successful transition.

The value-myth of retraining for a new profession. "Going back to school" is often thought to be a viable option for those considering a change in professions. Considered a necessary first step to prepare for a work transition—either to learn technical prerequisites or to acquire the supposed minimum educational requirements for entry into the profession—the logic is simple: Formal education substantiates your knowledge and bestows you with "validated" credibility. It also helps level the playing field, providing you with the same advantage as other applicants who flaunt a formal education.

The truth? While there are exceptions—for example, law and medicine—in most cases, you'll be better off landing an internship or taking a part-time job to break into a new industry. You'll learn the details first-hand and make valuable contacts that can help boost your career in the long term. Conversely, in a school environment, the focus is on a much broader base of knowledge (a curriculum), some of which (most of which?) turns out to be unimportant or unrelated to your eventual success.

Here's a short cautionary story to illustrate the point.

During my sophomore year at Arizona Western College, I needed a part-time job to help pay for expenses. One of my instructors suggested I obtain a commercial radio license. He'd had one for years and worked every weekend babysitting the remote transmitter of a local television station.

I studied the course material, drove to the FCC office in San Diego, and took the test. I'd had my license for less than a month when a local radio station (KVOY) called the college wanting to know if any of the students held a commercial radio license. They needed a part-time DJ for night and weekend work. Out of the entire student population, two were licensed. The station put both of us to work that same week.

Neither of us had any experience in broadcasting. I expected several weeks of training before finding myself sitting in front of a live microphone.

I was wrong.

The training was completed in a single afternoon—six hours of on ON-AIR, LIVE work. I read from prepared copy and was told which button to push and when to push it. After the first hour, the DJ providing the training began leaving the booth. At first, he was gone for a minute or two. Then ten minutes. Then half an hour. If I got into trouble, I was to make sure the mic was off and yell for help. At the end of the day, he told me my first paid shift started the next day. *And I would do it alone.*

A few months later, that weekend job grew into a full-time position, and that summer, I did the afternoon drive-time slot, from noon to six pm, six days a week.

The point of the story?

It comes three years later, after I'd moved to Denver to start my job with Acme Corp. One evening, I was visiting with a young couple who lived in the same apartment complex. The husband worked a full-time job and was also going to a private trade school—*to learn how to become a radio broadcaster.*

He'd been at it for two years, had spent thousands of dollars on tuition, and was nearing the end of his training. Even so, he didn't have his commercial license—yet. His "advisor" had told him the test preparation required "specialized training," consisting of several additional classes he would need to take after completing the operations part of the course. As he proudly boasted about his future goals—becoming a radio DJ personality—he admitted to having no idea about the current job prospects or how long it might be before he was finally working in the industry. However, he was sure his advanced education would shoot him right to the top of the business.

I hesitated to tell him about my experience at KVOY. I would be sticking a pin in his life-bubble. But I eventually decided a dose of reality might help balance all the hype and sales pitches he'd been listening to—and paying for—over the last two years.

His reaction? In short, he couldn't believe it. He'd been told the profession was extremely competitive, and the only way to ensure consideration from a potential employer was to have a professional broadcasting degree.

And yet, my personal experience offered proof of other ways into the industry—much quicker and less expensive ways.

The moral of the story is simple: Formal education is not necessarily an assurance of admission into a new profession. It rarely—if ever—guarantees a job or even a leg up on the competition. And compared to actual experience, a formal or traditional education can often be more of a detour than a direct route to accomplishing your career goals.

The advantages of *"doing now, learning now."* There have always been two ways to achieve a goal. The first way is to follow the rules, read the books, stand in line, respect the process and procedure, and invest enough time for others to bestow you with personal credibility.

The second is called *leapfrogging*—find an opportunity that puts you as close to the action as possible, and then jump in. Don't worry about the low pay or the fact that you're taking an entry position. You're gaining on-the-job experience. You'll learn about the industry *from the inside,* and most important, you'll make valuable connections that can help you move up.

(Author's note: I credit Robert Ringer with the term and concept of *Leapfrogging*. Although it may seem like an obvious extension of common sense, the process offers a practical counterpoint to K. Anders Ericsson's rule—popularized by Malcolm Gladwell—that advocates 10,000 hours of deliberate practice being required before one can expect success, or in Gladwell's words, "world-class in any field.")

Even if you plan to move from employee to entrepreneur, the principle of "leapfrogging" is the same. For example, I know some folks who began pursuing their goal of franchise ownership by taking night classes to learn accounting, marketing, and business management. I also know a few who went to work at an actual franchise location. They may have started behind the counter, cleaning the bathrooms, or driving a delivery truck, but they learned the business from the ground up, inside-out.

Which group of people do you think owns a franchise today? Of those I kept track of, a large percentage of the "book learners" ended up staying with their existing job or going back to their old profession. Those that jumped in and learned the business "hands-on" are counting their money as franchise owners.

If you're contemplating a career change that involves switching industries, determine the minimum professional or legal requirements for the job, and pursue those. Otherwise, spend time on what matters, in an actual work environment. You'll learn which tasks have the highest priority and how to make sure they're done right.

For example, do you want to sell real estate? Get a license and find a broker or team leader to be your mentor, *while you're on the job.*

Want to build custom homes? Get a job with a general contractor who specializes in new home construction. You may have to push a broom for six months or spend most of your time walking permits through the city's building and safety department, but at the end of a year, you'll know far more about the actual *business* of construction, including the priority of making a profit, than the majority of new graduates with a degree in construction management.

What about making a transition to a high-tech industry? The cutting edge of technology-based businesses generally changes faster than the associated course curriculum available through a traditional university. Learn what you need to know from online courses, blogs, and publications. Unless you're going to pursue pure research, a potential employer will be looking at more than your tech background and formal education. Attitude, initiative, professional goals, and personality have always been important to employers, and often make the deciding difference in getting the job you really want.

Chapter Twenty-Three
When the Axe Falls Unexpectedly ...

You show up for work a few minutes early, just like you have for the last five years. After pouring a cup of coffee, you head for your desk. And then you see it . . . A hand-written message, saying your boss needs to meet with you as soon as you arrive. It's a bit out of the ordinary, but you grab your notepad and head for her office. You're surprised when she stands to greet you, especially when she shakes your hand—you just saw her yesterday. You notice she seems unsettled, more businesslike than usual.

And then she begins:

"You've been a real asset to the company, and the years you've spent here have been good years. But with the reorganization, we've had to make some changes, and unfortunately, your position is being eliminated. I'm sorry to see this happen, but I know someone with your talent won't be out of the game for long. Take the rest of the day to tie up loose ends and check with the HR department to make arrangements for your severance, the transfer of your health insurance, your 401K . . . ."

The rest of it hits you as a dull roar, a blur of words you can't process. The phrase, "your position is being eliminated," keeps repeating inside your head.

You suddenly realize the boss has finished speaking, and she's waiting for your response.

You feel like you've been attacked. Blindsided!

You're filled with questions . . . *Why me? Why now? Why wasn't I a part of the discussion before they made the decision? Can't we talk about this?*

You feel the anger building. This is not only unfair, but it's also illegal—or it should be. You want to lash out, tell the boss exactly how you feel.

But DON'T do it.

Even though your brain is reeling, you must respond *as a professional*. Here's why: The first words out of your mouth—your initial reaction after receiving the news of your termination—are the ones that will be remembered. Yes, you're ready to explode, but you must temper your reaction with perspective.

If you're on the verge of losing it, simply say, "I understand." Then add, "I appreciate it coming from you. We've had a good relationship, and I know it's never easy for a supervisor to terminate someone."

Like it or not, you must do everything you can to preserve your relationship with your boss. She is a vital source of recommendation. And although you want to vent your anger and frustration, you'll gain nothing and end up hurting yourself professionally. At the time, it may be difficult to evaluate her potential influence on your future career—especially through a cloud of disappointment and anger—but her recommendation is one of the few remaining assets the company can provide. So don't blow it.

Your post-employment relationship with your employer must be about you. If selected for termination, you must continue to present yourself as a professional during the exit phase and beyond. And that means no flipping off the boss as you turn in your company car keys, or including a letter of dissent and accusation with your exit documents. Any negative input from you will become ammunition that management and HR can use to torpedo your future career, especially if you stay in the same industry.

Your next move? Remember, management often does the wrong things to the wrong people. Whether you were caught in a widely-cast net of layoffs and downsizing, or singled out for termination because of a comment you made to the VP's wife at the Christmas party, your stellar past performance and contributions to the company won't buy you another minute behind your desk. The die is cast. You're leaving, and even though you didn't see it coming, it's time to concentrate on your professional future.

If you find yourself in this situation, make two personal commitments:

1. Mentally leave your old job behind. Yes, you're moving on, and you're taking plenty of valuable assets with you—your experience, your professional and personal contacts, and the knowledge you gained from your employer. And you're going to put those to good use.

2. Use every advantage in the time you have left to make your transition to a new employer as financially and emotionally stable as possible.

You may not be allowed to exploit the second suggestion. It's not unusual for a dismissed employee to be required to leave the premises immediately. For reasons having to do with preventing intellectual property thief, preservation of the workplace atmosphere, rumor control, and reducing wrongful termination lawsuits, the immediate removal of a terminated employee has become common.

Overcoming the "Damaged Goods" stigma. While the actual impact on your future job prospects will depend on your previous accomplishments, specialization, and the level of supply versus demand for talent within your industry, being terminated without notice generally damages your negotiating strength in seeking a new position. It means you'll have to present yourself to potential new employers as someone who is out of work—someone who *needs* a job. Losing the leverage of being currently employed means there's no need to match your current salary because you don't have one. And asking a potential employer to sweeten the benefits package is off the table because you don't have an existing one as a comparison. From the perspective of a new employer, you're talent at large, on the street, needing a job.

If you find yourself in this situation, try to buy some consideration in the form of "non-resident" employment status. Tell your supervisor you understand the need to maintain the uniform enforcement of company policy. However, you would like the company to consider moving your official date of termination thirty to sixty days into the future. This will allow you to seek other employment under the guise of being currently employed. Assure the HR department that granting your request will not affect your severance or the need for any additional compensation, and in fact, would be extremely beneficial in mitigating the negative personal impact of their decision to terminate you. (Translation? You won't sue for wrongful termination.)

Your chances of being granted those extra thirty to sixty days? It's a long shot. Less than one in twenty, with the odds slightly improved if you were working at an executive management position. As we've discussed, HR can be a heartless bastard when dealing with exiting employees, but if you're leaving with a clean, productive record, and you've got some friends in management, you might be the exception.

Another way to reclaim some of your leverage in the eyes of a new and potential employer? Start a consulting company. (I hear the moans and groans in the background. Yes, I know some of you are already rejecting the idea. But before you dismiss it completely, hear me out.)

Begin by choosing a generic company name that doesn't indicate or infer a specific industry or product. And don't use proper nouns. For example, I did consulting work for a company called, International Communication & Business Marketing (ICBM), which allowed me to move my marketing pitch from one industry to another without needing to rationalize the company's identity or specialization.

So for now, we'll call your new company, XYZ Consulting, Inc.

"But wait!" you say. "This side trip will divert me from my real goal of replacing my occupation. I'm not interested in consulting work or starting my own company. I need to find a new job!"

Don't worry. In this situation, you're the boss. You're in charge. You choose how much time, energy, and effort you put into your new creation—as well as how much you get out of it. Also keep in mind the primary purpose of creating a consulting company is to give the impression of making a seamless transition from your old job to a new one—an indication of your value on the open market. In fact, a new employer is going to have to "steal" you away from XYZ with an even more lucrative offer than they might have made before you left your old job to work for XYZ.

Is this misrepresentation? Not if you're offering your services to the market.

First, you need to give your company legitimacy with a credible public image. At a minimum, that means a website with several pages of appropriate "industry-speak," along with contact information and the location of a physical headquarters. There are companies offering this "headquartering" service, including mail forwarding, phone answering, and a legitimate-looking office or storefront presence. You can also consider using a relative's address or that of a past business associate who understands your situation.

Earlier, I talked about the risks of leaving a new job too soon and being labeled a *job-hopper,* someone who is unreliable and unpredictable—not someone a potential new employer wants to hire if they believe there's a risk of an early exit. Doesn't the possibility of doing a short-term stint as a consultant carry some of the same negative implications?

Remember, we're talking about representing your professional status as a consultant. You're not an employee, nor are you unemployed. You're a specialized expert in your industry—someone who could be a valuable asset to any employer looking for top-notch talent. It's a simple shift in perspective, and it can give you the leverage you need to become a company's "first-choice" when they make their final cut.

During your stint as a consultant, are you going to perform any actual work? Depending on what you do, it's very possible you could pick up some freelance work. For example, if you have a marketing or sales background, you could offer your services to vendors, OEMs, and sales organizations that sell products and services in markets familiar to you. If you're an accountant, offer to set up accounting software for new and small businesses.

"This sounds like a lot of work. Is setting up an XYZ Corporation really worth all the effort?"

It could make a big difference in how potential employers perceive your value. Here's how a job search performed by a full-time consultant outweighs one undertaken by an unemployed job-seeker.

- You have immediate credibility. Someone who is employed is always perceived as more valuable than one who is not.

- You have an existing financial platform (your compensation) from which to negotiate a new position.

- Your termination from your past employer is not the most recent event in your professional history, and therefore, does not have the same degree of negative influence. Yes, some employers may assume you began doing consulting work to generate income until you find a new position. But even so, the fact that you're currently working goes a long way in reducing the stigma of being previously terminated.

I know the option of creating a consulting company won't "feel right" for everyone. However, if you see the advantages, here are a few suggestions to get started:

Offer your services. Most job functions are directly transferable to the status of an independent contractor, so whatever you did in your previous job, you can offer to do it free-lance. Establish a competitive rate and advertise your services online and in industry trade publications. Remember, finding a new "forever" job could take some time. Based on your previous position, income, and industry, it could easily take a month for every ten thousand dollars in compensation you expect to replace. Offering yourself as an independent contractor will allow you to pick up a few bucks in the interim, and you might even find a permanent position with one of your new clients.

Look and act the part. Have some business cards printed. Create a letterhead and have a logo designed by a graphics artist (try Fiverr.com – modifying a stock design to meet your needs usually runs less than $50.00). Also, add a new phone number to your cell phone that you can answer with the company name.

Write an article about some aspect of your industry that is a popular or perennial favorite in trade journals. It will give you immediate credibility and may even produce interest from company recruiters with a subsequent offer of employment. Be sure to list your credentials and a short bio at the end of the article, including your current position with XYZ Consulting, Inc. Any email responses or comments you receive should be followed up quickly and professionally, knowing there's the possibility of turning one of them into a job offer.

What if your "side-venture" takes on a life of its own, becoming so time-consuming that it impedes your job search?

Good question. The answer is completely up to you. Is your new company making money? If you're becoming too busy with consulting work to conduct a job search, you're probably generating some income. Is it enough to consider setting the job search aside and putting all of your time and resources into making a go of XYZ?

As I said before, this approach is not for everyone. Creating a new business entity as a tool to make your talents and experience more marketable may seem overwhelming. And for some, it may be counterproductive. If so, stick to a conventional job search. You don't need the additional stress.

What about using a headhunter? A headhunter is a company or individual who recruits talented people and matches them with employers who are specifically looking to fill a vacancy. The headhunter charges a fee, usually paid by the hiring company.

There's certainly nothing wrong with letting a placement agency know you're available. Base your choice of an agency on the financial terms of their services. Any agency requiring an upfront fee or retainer should be avoided. An ethical and effective headhunter makes their money from *placements.* Their clients are the companies who hire them to find new talent. And while there are exceptions, the hiring company usually pays the agency's placement fee.

Be aware of so-called "hybrid" services that charge a fee to update your resume or process your application and place you into their system. Sometimes these charges are called "administrative" fees and can run anywhere from a few hundred dollars to several thousand. While you may consider paying the smaller amount—to offset the company's initial processing costs—never pay a large fee to a placement company that promises to *make best efforts* to find a job for you. If their income stream is based on hopeful candidates, and they collect their money upfront, there's little incentive to place anyone.

If you're tempted by a sales pitch from a hybrid agency, ask for the names of specific companies that hired their job candidates in the last three months. Then ask how many total placements they've made in the previous twelve months (in the salary range you're looking for). If they balk, or can't give you a specific number, avoid them like the plague.

There's one more caveat to working with a placement agency: Some portion of the placement fee (or the entire fee!) may become your financial responsibility if you leave your new employer prematurely. Often called an "early departure penalty," this condition will be spelled out in your hiring contract, and should not only define the expiration or term, but permissible exceptions, such as health reasons or unforeseen circumstances that might prevent you from continuing your employment.

Make sure you understand every word of any contract containing an early departure penalty. If you don't, ask an employment attorney to translate. If you're uncomfortable with the terms, explain your reasons to the hiring manager, and ask if the stipulation can be revised to reflect a more realistic (and fair) pre-requisite to your hiring.

When dealing with a placement agency, don't forget that the headhunter works for the hiring company, not you.

Although a credible agency will represent you in the best possible light, the real selling is up to you. And that means promoting not only your specific skill set, but also your personality, attitude, and your willingness to meet the needs of a prospective employer.

A head-hunter makes money by successfully matching prospective employees with companies willing to pay the placement fee. They will not endanger their professional reputation by recommending a "ho-hum" candidate. A placement agency wants its clients (the companies that hire them) to think of them as a supplier of exceptional talent, so that means you've got to sell yourself exceptionally well.

Always have a Plan B. Regardless of the direction you've chosen for your career, always give yourself the benefit of an organized *Plan B*. Think of it as a contingency plan that's ready to implement if and when you need it. Even if your career is on target and you believe your position with the company is "solid as a rock," going through the exercise of formulating a transition plan will help you identify and focus on your career and life priorities. You'll also gain a greater sense of confidence, knowing you have a strategy for changing employers—even if it happens unexpectedly. Here are a few suggestions to get you started:

1. **Establish a financial timeline.** If your income from your current position stops, how long can you survive financially, based on your resources? Don't just estimate or speculate based on a best-case situation. These should be quantifiable measurements. For example, how long will your savings last if you lose your job? How long can you count on a severance package? Never evaluate a severance package in the same way as your savings account or other cash-equivalent investments. Your personal assets are in your possession and/or under your control. A severance package is neither. Until

severance money is received, either by a company check that clears your bank, or is irrevocably transferred from the company's account to yours, you can't rely on it. Companies change their policy. They reverse previous decisions. They default on previous agreements. So consider any severance you receive as a bonus. And if you're given the option of a lump-sum payout or a monthly check, always take the lump-sum upfront.

2. **Set up a working draft of possible courses of action and their probable results.** This can take the form of an outline, a list, or a logic flow-chart. Include short term options as well as long-term career goals. Keep your plan current by adding new opportunities and eliminating old ones that no longer exist. This kind of planning can be extremely helpful when dealing with an unanticipated layoff, transfer, or early retirement option, especially when emotion and the overwhelming nature of the circumstances can leave you distraught or on the edge of panic.

3. **Give your brain the best environment in which to work.** This means taking a walk when you hit a wall. The old adage of allowing your mind to "sleep on it" actually helps your brain process the data and generate possible solutions. Realize that confusion is the mind's natural "holding" state until an answer is reached. Neuro-linguistic research has long held that "feeling confused" indicates your brain is actively working on a solution. If an answer doesn't eventually present itself, it's usually a sign you need additional information about one or more of the options under consideration.

4. **Evaluate the advice from others based on what they have to gain or lose from your decision.** Remember, the opinions and input of others carry no guarantee of making you happy or providing you with satisfaction in the long term. That's up to you. Relying too much on the advice of others may provide a scapegoat for an unsatisfying future, but you're the

one who will have to deal with the results of making choices that are ultimately wrong for you.

5. **Maintain as many "normal" activities in your life as possible.** If you usually go to the park with your dog on Tuesdays and Fridays, make the effort to continue. If you typically set aside Sunday afternoons to tend to a garden, or read the next chapter in a favorite novel, or play a round of golf, try to maintain that schedule. Life-change is best accomplished by altering one situation at a time. Keep as many of your positive life rituals as possible, knowing this can provide a sense of stability as you explore new options during this phase of your life.

Chapter Twenty-Four
Time to Strike Out on Your Own?

Staying motivated and focused on our work is a constant challenge, especially after settling into the day-to-day routine. After a few years, it's not unusual to feel bored and frustrated over the sameness of the work. We question the decisions of management—or lack of them. We wonder if we're ever going to move up. And then there's the issue of money—having our income limited by budgets and functional compensation programs can make us question our economic future. It's enough to discourage even the most dedicated employee.

Most of us shake it off and go back to work. *I'm building a great retirement, and I've got financial security here.* At least that's what we tell ourselves.

Another year passes. It doesn't get worse, but it doesn't get better. Same rocks. Same hammer.

Determined to elevate our status as a viable candidate for an upper management position, we flaunt our accomplishments during our annual evaluation—and receive a six percent raise. Just like the year before. Just like everyone else.

Then one afternoon we're sitting in our car on the freeway, and it happens—the trumpets sound, the clouds part, and the answer appears in a shining blaze of insight:

I should be working for myself!

Sounds good, right? But before you turn in your resignation and order new business cards, you need to think long and hard about your motives. Yes, entrepreneurship can—about fifty percent of the time—produce real advantages for those willing to take the risk. But constant euphoria is not one of them.

Unfortunately, the first lesson many new entrepreneurs learn is that they've traded corporate boredom for financial stress and logistical overwhelm. And if they lack the resiliency to handle it, they typically find themselves wishing for the good old days back at ABC corporation, where they could call the legal department to take care of contractual issues and liability concerns, and where the graphics department could turn out a new web page or print ad the same day, and where an administrative assistant handled their correspondence and paperwork. And don't forget, all that "backup" infrastructure was ready and available without worrying about the expense of maintaining it.

Before giving up your job, make sure you're leaving for the "right" reasons. The need to strike out on your own is a very personal decision, and it's typically driven by a wide variety of motivations. Even so, there are several commonalities among those who have made a successful transition to entrepreneurship. Here's my top ten:

1. **They have perseverance.** When you own your own business, you take the failures—big and small—personally, but you process them with perspective. Giving up is not an option. If every little hiccup sends you into a tailspin, you probably don't have the tenacity to be your own boss. Entrepreneurs are willing to work until they get it done. Whether it's a website, a presentation, or preparing a complex estimate for a potential client, entrepreneurs understand the necessity of meeting a deadline, and they often work nights and weekends to make sure nothing falls through the cracks. No, you don't necessarily have to be a workaholic to become a successful entrepreneur, but it doesn't hurt. Keep in mind that despite having intentions of maintaining a balanced life, many entrepreneurs sacrifice their health and personal relationships to ensure the success of their business— especially in the beginning stages, when they typically start their venture as a one-person show.

2. **They have a grasp of the big picture.** They understand the industry inside-out. They know the motivations and buying criteria of their customers. They know how much it costs to manufacture the product or provide the service they sell, right down to the penny. And they know how that compares to the competition.

3. **They are goal-oriented and use time-management skills religiously**. They know how to separate the important from the trivial and make sure they accomplish the highest priority tasks first. They also know that nothing is cast in stone.

4. **They enjoy what they do.** They like the people as well as the products or services associated with the industry. They know that doing it only for the money is a fast route to burnout. They also know that building a successful company takes time and dedication, not to mention the investment and re-investment of personal capital. Unless you believe in what you're doing, the problems, setbacks, and outright failures will send you running for the nearest job-placement service.

5. **They're not afraid to break the rules.** They know that circumventing traditional procedures and processes is often the key to finding success, especially when it comes to beating the competition. Many times this means thinking *way* outside the box. For example, when my wife and I started a home-based photography business, we mounted an expensive laser-etched wood sign displaying our company name and logo next to the front door. And while we lacked the first-impression credibility of our store-front competition, the sign helped convey the idea that we were every bit as professional. However, within two weeks, we received a complaint from city zoning—we were in violation of the signage regulations. Specifically, we were advertising a business within a residential community, which was strictly against city ordinances. Not wanting to give up the positive impression our professional signage conveyed to clients,

we needed an alternative. The following week, we purchased a white Chevy Astro cargo van and hired a graphics artist to paint the name of our business, our logo, and phone number on both sides. The result was a high quality mobile billboard that made a far larger impression than our original sign ever could have. We left the van parked in our driveway so it was the first thing our clients saw as they approached from the street. And the best part? It was legal.

6. **They have great rapport and presentation skills**. They can make a professional presentation to a group of one or one-hundred. They know how to listen, ask the right questions, and solve customer problems. *In other words, they know how to sell.*

7. **They make new connections easily**. They are natural networkers, promoters, and marketers, and are comfortable with social media. They immediately follow up with new contacts and periodically touch base to keep the relationship active. For example, my current real estate partner has a Christmas card list with over seven thousand names. Every year, everyone on the list gets a hand-signed card. Does it make a difference? Absolutely, especially when it's a part of the regular effort he makes to contact each person by email or phone at least six times throughout the year.

8. **They take calculated risks.** They objectively weigh the risk-reward ratio of any new expenditure and won't hesitate to put their savings on the line when it makes sense.

9. **They don't see the transition from employee to entrepreneur as an earth-shattering move.** In fact, they often view it as a natural evolution of their career. Even as employees, they harbored an entrepreneurial spirit. Most were already thinking in "maverick-mode" long before they left their employer, perhaps operating a small side business or providing non-competitive consulting services.

10. **Their business radar is always "on."** Continually looking for ways to improve existing procedures and make their business more profitable, they're also on the lookout for new opportunities. If they can't take advantage of them, they refer them to non-competitive associates who can.

The above list is far from complete, but it's representative of the mindset and typical skill-set most people need to make a successful transition from employee to business owner. Yes, I'm aware of the few brilliant eccentrics that "seed" a new enterprise solely with their research or original design, and then use others to perform the peripheral tasks. But for every introverted, digital game designer, there are hundreds of well-rounded, communicative, business-savvy individuals who built their operation from the ground up, doing whatever was necessary to move toward eventual—and more probable—success.

Let's Look at the Numbers . . .

The idea that financial independence is just waiting for anyone willing to make the commitment and do the work is a compelling argument. And based on such straightforward logic, we should see a steady and ever-increasing number of new business start-ups annually.

However, the facts tell us otherwise.

Historically, the number of full-time workers starting or running their own businesses is a consistent 13 percent (source: Global Entrepreneurship Monitor). This may jump a point or two in the short term, but after factoring in the number of new businesses still operating after five years, the number doesn't change much.

(Yes, other sources—the Freelancers Union, Entrepreneur, and MBO Partners for example—claim much higher percentages, often alleging as much as one-third of the workforce is engaging in some kind of self-employment. But these higher percentages often include work-at-home or at-a-distance employees, as well as those employed for term projects as independent contractors. These numbers may also be influenced by those who generate a second or side income by working in the so-called "gig" economy. For those reasons, I've chosen to focus on data obtained from conservative, longer-term sources.)

The five-year business failure rate tells an even more sobering story. According to the SBA (Small Business Administration) and the Bureau of Labor Statistics, about 20 percent of all startups fail in the first year. At the end of two years, a third are gone. And after five years, only fifty percent will remain. These numbers have remained relatively consistent over the last twenty years, and surprisingly, are not radically affected by the general economy.

These numbers are a cruel reminder of the inescapable risk of being an entrepreneur. Start your own business, and there's a damn good chance you're going to fail. In fact, it's a fifty-fifty proposition by year five.

With that in mind, here's the question every budding entrepreneur needs to ask themselves . . .

Knowing that after working and investing your capital in your own business for five-years, you face a fifty percent chance of failure, does it still make sense to give up your professional relationship with a large, financially stable and successful company?

For the sake of argument, let's say you're willing to take the risk. Then ask yourself this: By comparison, where you will be in five-years on *both* career tracks—maintaining your corporate career versus pursuing an entrepreneurial path? Obviously, you can't project the outcome of either track with absolute certainty. But you can extrapolate—based on the experiences of others in the same industry—the probable likelihood of success.

If you make an honest and realistic assessment of your resources, the projected expansion of your chosen industry, the competition, and a conservative estimate of how long it will take before your new business becomes profitable, you'll likely come to the same three conclusions shared by successful employees who have risen to the very top of their industry:

- **A job is a financial asset.** It's the source of your income and livelihood. It funds your current lifestyle, your investment portfolio, and your future retirement. And coincidently, it provides the opportunity to explore alternative business interests without the financial pressure of needing to generate an immediate income from your "side-gig."

- **You are never more valuable (to another employer) than when you are currently employed.** When you're ready to make a strategic career move, there's no better leverage than being currently employed. It means new companies must "court" you, ostensibly offering you an increase in compensation, and often, more authority and recognition to motivate you to leave your current position.

- **Your "insider" status enhances your access to the movers and shakers of your industry.** You are part of the picture, and you have the privilege of looking at it from the inside. An outsider will seldom have the opportunity to establish the number of professional and personal relationships that a successful employee can. And it's the quality of those relationships that can help you advance to the very top of your profession.

I want to make it clear that I'm not suggesting the corporate environment is the only viable method of finding career success. Instead, I'm advocating you make an extensive and cautious evaluation of any new career opportunity, especially if it involves a radical change in the source and reliability of your income.

Here's the bottom line on entrepreneurship. If you find several of the typical entrepreneurial characteristics out of sync with your personality, work ethic, personal values, or stress tolerance, you're probably better off—and will be happier in the long run— if you remain a company man or woman.

Chapter Twenty-Five
The New Rules for the Corporate Maverick

In writing this book, my goal was to answer the question, "How can working for a corporation realistically fit into a larger life-plan of success, independence, and career satisfaction?"

I'll summarize the answer with what I consider to be the seven most important cornerstones of a personal success plan based on utilizing a corporate career as the marketing centerpiece for your skill and talent. In short, it's a self-directed approach to maximizing your financial success while realizing a sense of satisfaction and self-worth from your career—no matter what kind of work you do.

1. **Make a place for yourself.** There is no such thing as an "indispensable employee." Management will recognize outstanding work and reward you to the extent the system allows. However, never let yourself believe you're in total control of your destiny when you work for a large company. Respect—and use—the political bureaucracy and the chain of authority. It's the fastest way to accelerate to the top.

2. **Be aware of new opportunities within the company and when appropriate, throw your hat into the ring.** Make management aware of your ultimate job goals within the company. If you feel you're not moving up as rapidly as you should, discuss the situation with your supervisor and identify the short-falls in performance, knowledge, or experience preventing you from receiving a promotion. Then determine—with your supervisor's approval—how to best correct the deficiencies. Include a timeline for reviewing your progress. This process is as much about making the company aware that you're ready to handle more responsibility as it is personal preparation.

3. **Consider your job a business that can become as successful as you choose to make it.** Your "job" is the method by which you offer your professional services to the market. It's also the way you receive compensation for your work. And just like any business owner, your attitude, dedication, expertise, and experience will, to a large degree, determine how profitable your business becomes. "Riding out the years" is not an option for those who want to be truly successful. Improving, learning, and becoming more effective are the hallmarks of those consistently recognized as being on the cutting edge of their industry.

4. **Keep your "life-plan" confidential.** No matter how tempting it may be to reveal your plan, or how much you want to brag about your career strategy and independent mindset, it's far most useful—and powerful—to keep it to yourself. Otherwise, every move you make will be suspect, leaving others to wonder if your actions are influenced by ulterior motives—namely, putting your interests first and the company's second. While that's exactly the case, announcing it to the world will not serve your best interests.

5. **Create an investment strategy that will eventually provide you with economic independence.** This is not optional. A portion of every paycheck should be allocated to a 401K or equivalent tax-deferred investment plan. Diversify only into investments that you understand. A common strategy, for example, is to contribute the maximum to a 401K while investing in conservative growth stocks and rental real estate.

6. **If the entrepreneurial "bug" continues to gnaw at you, consider a side business.** This can take the form of a non-competitive consulting service, the online sale of instructional material, photography services, writing, or the buying and selling of non-perishable goods through eBay or

Esty. In all cases, your side gig should be unrelated to your main job, and there should never be any common customer overlap. Above all, your involvement in outside, profit-generating activities must never be revealed to anyone associated with your employer. And that includes the company's customers, vendors, suppliers, distributors, and yes, even the UPS gal. Your employer must never discover that the control of your time, energy, and attention is not exclusively theirs.

7. **Immunize yourself against false loyalty.** Your job and the opportunity it represents are only valuable if it serves your plan in the long term. Always be aware of the advantages of moving to a new or different company to improve your compensation, life-work balance, and to gain a more positive and rewarding work experience.

Epilogue

I'd like to end this book with a blog post I wrote some time back that has been reprinted on LinkedIn, Thrive Global, and Medium. It continues to be one of the most popular posts on my blog, www.SuccessPoint360.com. It's called . . .

A Note to My Nephew

I have a nephew who reminds me of myself; the me from thirty years ago—aggressive, wanting to excel, battling the other "bright boys" also competing on the fast track, and hoping to score a cushy corner office on the tenth floor of the corporate office.

I have no idea if he'll read this. And if he does, if he'll recognize the similarities—where I've come from and where he's likely headed. I hope he'll see the commonalities, and understand how quickly they can become consequences.

For the last several years, he's been following the path laid out for him—the same path that's lured several generations of young men and women before him, hoping it leads them to the mother lode.

But just in case it doesn't—just in case the promises made by supervisors and managers don't come to pass, or budget restrictions, company politics, and buy-outs suddenly derail his timeline for advancement—I'd like to offer a few suggestions:

Temper your enthusiasm for your job with the understanding that you're following a plan made by someone else. And other people's plans can change in the blink of an eye. There's always the possibility you could be caught in the crossfire and end up as another casualty of downsizing, or corporate culture-shift, or mid-management reduction. It can happen with very little warning, so . . .

Be prepared. Not only with six months of living expenses and an updated resume, but with a heightened state of awareness, to recognize the warning signs, to take action before the first salvo hits, to take full advantage of the transitional time when you're forced to make an alternative career move.

Always make a positive impression. How others perceive you is often more important than what you accomplish. Much of your success in a corporate environment will depend not only on what you actually do, but what your superiors think of you. The corporation is one of those places where knowing the location of your boss's favorite restaurant, his drink of choice, and his preference in sports teams can have as much impact on your performance review as your actual achievements.

Realize that every successful career requires a commitment—from both sides. Bringing everything you have to a business relationship is great, but it must be a two-way street. If it's one-sided for too long, trust and loyalty become contaminated with doubt and suspicion. The commitment you make to your job is always conditional, with the unspoken contingency that the other side will also live up to their promises. In this case, the company wants your loyalty, dedication, and a level of consistent performance that meets or exceeds their expectations. In turn, they offer compensation and the potential for a rewarding future. Make sure neither of you ends up shortchanged.

Understand there will be days when you'll feel you've been taken advantage of, unappreciated, or flat-out

snubbed in favor of someone else. The key is to know if the situation is a symptom of a larger problem, or if you're misinterpreting the circumstances with short term vision. In working for any large company, longevity results from successful compromise. During your career, you'll be asked to do things that seem silly, wasteful, unnecessary, or downright stupid. You may be used as a scapegoat, and then expected to respond with a professional, "company-first" attitude.

Working for an employer means you must pursue their goals and objectives. Sometimes they'll mesh with your own. Many times, they won't. But you do it anyway, because the company compensates you for it, and in the long term, you're counting on the rewards outweighing the sacrifice. Whatever you do, avoid the temptation to complain, lash out at co-workers, or storm out of the office. Remember, tomorrow could be *your* day to be recognized for excellence. But if you respond with an emotional outburst, I can guarantee it won't be.

Remember, your every move is being watched. You are always being judged and evaluated. "Is this guy a company man? Is he worth keeping? Should we consider her for promotion?" These are the questions management is constantly asking—about you. Make sure the answers reflect a constant stream of yes's. And that's true even if you don't plan on staying with the company in the long-term.

Consider your job to be one of your most valuable assets. In spite of the popular trend toward entrepreneurship, there is nothing "wrong" with being an employee. Many employees are intelligent—even brilliant— hard-working individuals who are happiest when working on a specific task or project. Often doing their best work when it's defined in terms of a goal or preferred outcome, they appreciate the organizational discipline a large company can offer. As an employee, there are no divisional budgets to balance, and no corporate taxes to pay or profit margins to worry about unless it falls under the specifics of their job responsibility.

If you see yourself on the other side of the parking lot, belonging to that group of competitive, politically-savvy fast-trackers who covet a vice-presidency, access to the company jet, and their picture in the annual report, then be ready to do whatever your company asks of you, because as a "company man or woman," your life must be decidedly unbalanced, with your first priority squarely focused on the needs of your employer. You will need to prove your value with unquestioning loyalty while secretly managing your personal ambitions. And most important, you'll deal with the sobering reality that you walk a tight-rope of accountability, requiring you to meet the subjective needs of the company's most powerful and influential—any one of whom will not hesitate to replace you if you fall short of their expectations.

I'm going to keep a good thought and hope my nephew reads this. Maybe it will motivate him to ask a question or two, and then determine what's true for him. If by chance it raises a few caution flags, even better. I hope it leaves him better prepared to navigate around the confusing and often destructive detours that waste our time and often leave us feeling bitter and full of regret—especially as we get older. If nothing else, I hope he realizes his career—regardless of where or how he spends it—is only one aspect of his life. Granted, it's an important one, but no more so than time spent with family or taking care of his health.

Most of all, I hope he enjoys the journey.

About the Author

Roger A. Reid, Ph.D. is the founder/host of the **Success Point 360 Podcast** and author of *Speak Up! A Step-by-Step Method to Conquer Your Fears and Give an Amazing Speech*. A certified NLP trainer with degrees in engineering and business, Roger draws on his background as a fourteen-year corporate employee, business owner, and management consultant to help others achieve higher levels of career success and personal fulfillment in the real world.

If you have a question, comment, or would like additional information about anything in this book, you can contact Roger by email at Roger@RogerReid.com. You can also read his blog posts and articles, and listen to his weekly podcast by visiting www.SuccessPoint360.com

Success Point 360 Podcast – https://SuccessPoint360.com
LinkedIn – https://www.linkedin.com/in/RogerAReid
Medium – https://medium.com/@RogerAReidPhD
Facebook – https://facebook.com/RogerReidPhD
Twitter – https://twitter.com/SuccessPoint360

Speak Up by Roger A. Reid

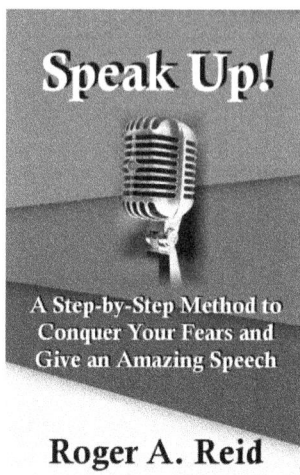

Available from Amazon

Speak Up! A Step-by-Step Method to Conquer Your Fears and Give An Amazing Speech, is a powerful system of tools and techniques on how to tame your nerves and deliver your talk with skill and confidence.

Been asked by the boss to make a presentation to the company's sales team?

Concerned you'll end up tongue-tied when you speak at your best friend's wedding?

Worried you'll be called on to "say a few words" at your high school reunion?

Whether it's a short impromptu speech, a convention keynote, business presentation, or just saying a few words at a social gathering, this comprehensive guide outlines detailed methods for creating interesting and relevant speech content, how and when to use props, and proven ways to establish positive rapport with the audience.

Even spur of the moment situations—when you're taken by surprise with a spontaneous request to "say a few words"—are covered, with examples, formats, and templates that will leave others impressed with your ability to think on your feet while presenting your message with confidence and authority.

And for those ready to improve their speaking ability, the author includes advanced strategies on vocal technique and body language—everything you need to "stand and deliver," while leaving a memorable and lasting impression.

Here's an excerpt from the book:

PART ONE

Taming Your Nerves and Making All That Energy Work for You

You've seen them. Calm and collected, they rise from their chair and walk to the front of the room with an expression of absolute confidence. They take the mic, look out over the audience, and then . . . Magic.

The words just seem to flow.

These are the people who seem to know just what to say and how to say it—and they can do it in front of any size group. They don't appear to need preparation, and welcome any opportunity to speak. It's as if they've found the secret to being confident as well as eloquent when all eyes and ears are on them.

Want to know the truth? Ninety-nine percent of all public speakers admit to fighting a case of nerves when facing an audience—no matter how many presentations they've done. Some book authors have passed out at the podium, and many business owners outright admit they're scared to death as they step up to face the crowd. Some even relate personal stories of hiding in the bathroom until the last minute so no one can see them doing push-ups to calm a nervous stomach.

So when you see that guy or gal walk to the front of the room in complete confidence, the overwhelming probability is their stomach is doing flip-flips, their heart is pounding like a jack-hammer, and they're hoping no one can see the beads of sweat running down the back of their neck.

In truth, their collected and professional appearance is part of the presentation. In other words, they realize their speech starts from the very moment their name is called, and as they rise from the chair, it's already fully underway. By presenting an image of confidence, they're portraying a sense of personal authority that sets the mood for what comes next.

I know what you're thinking . . .

If professional speakers have to fight butterflies in *their* stomachs, how am I ever going to control my nerves to the point I can say something without looking like I'm scared to death?

It's all about getting those butterflies to fly in formation.

The Secret to Controlling Your Nerves

Speakers make great speeches not in spite of their nerves, *but because of them.* They've learned to harness all that nervous energy and use it to their advantage. In fact, most welcome the rush of adrenaline as they hear their name. They know how to channel and direct it to energize their presentation and to make them a better presenter than they could ever be without it.

As I said before, a rise in energy level just before giving any kind of performance is a common occurrence. Even after hundreds or even thousands of presentations, many of very best speakers admit to still having the jitters before walking on stage. As they hear their name called to take the microphone, they feel their pulse quicken, their stomach tighten—just like they did the very first time. But now, they not only expect it, they welcome it. In fact, they depend on that surge of nervous energy to insure their level of performance is enthusiastic, in-the-moment, and meets their standards of professional delivery.

And that's what you're going to learn, too.

While the intention of this guide is not to turn you into a professional toastmaster, don't be surprised if it does just that. It's designed to give you a flexible structure in which to prepare a public presentation—whether it's a formal event (like a wedding), or a spontaneous request "to say a few words" to your customers, fraternal organization, or church group. It will also give you the tools you need to be more comfortable when speaking in a work setting, whether you're the designated leader or a contributing member of the team.

How do you convert your fear into excitement? By assuring yourself you need that nervous energy to boost the delivery of your presentation. It becomes an expected and reliable tool to give you that something "extra" that makes people sit up and pay attention.

And yes, there are specific steps you can take to turn those feelings of dread into *positive energy and enthusiasm*.

- **Make sure you've prepared the content of your speech right down to the last pause and period.** That may sound like I'm pointing out the obvious, but you can't imagine the number of people who believe they can make their first speech by jotting down a few notes on some index cards and winging it. Unless they have previous experience in front of an audience, they typically end up forgetting half of what they planned to say, ramble through a disconnected thought or two, and fill in the embarrassing silence with lots of "ands" and "ah's." Worse, I've heard a few actually apologize by saying, "I wish I'd practiced more," or "Sorry I'm doing such a poor job at this."

Being prepared—knowing you're ready—raises your confidence. You can't fail because you can do it in your sleep. Even if your brain begins to shut down, your memory will feed the words to your mouth because you've practiced so many times it's become second nature.

The key is to practice until you can launch into your speech from any point in the beginning, middle, or end without needing to think about what came before or after. In other words, you know exactly what you're going to say by heart, and can deliver it on demand. How much practice is enough? Depends. Everyone is different. For me, the magic number is about fifty rehearsals. Yes, I could do it with less drill, but that degree of preparation gives me the latitude to stop, start, go off topic, accommodate a question from the audience, then resume my place in the presentation as if the interruption never happened—and do it with absolute confidence.

- **Don't forget to breath.** I discounted this advice for years, not understanding the connection between the body, brain, and the importance of deep, rhythmic breathing. Taking deep, controlled breaths is a relaxation technique inherent to most meditative practices. It can lower blood pressure, heart rate, and stress levels. Not surprisingly, irregular, shallow breathing can add additional stress, making your situation even worse. Incorporating a series of deep breaths during the final minutes prior to your presentation will provide you with a natural, easy-to-activate method of lowering your stress, calming your mind, and sharpening your mental reflexes. Remember to use it!

- **Imagine the worst that could happen and ask yourself, "What are the odds?"** I had a business colleague who approached each speaking opportunity with the idea that if everything went to hell—if he completely forgot what he was going to say and was booed off the stage—it wouldn't matter, because life would still go on. His friends would forgive him, strangers wouldn't care, and a week later, very few would even remember what happened. So in a worst case scenario, he would live to speak again. With this thought firmly in place, he would ask himself, "What are the odds of forgetting my presentation and looking like a complete idiot?" He knew they were about zero. Even experienced speakers will have an occasional memory lapse, but they fill in the missing information from the context of their subject, or simply move on to the next part of their speech. So the odds of a total mental meltdown are next to nil.

The outcome of this mind-game? Knowing his worst case performance was too remote a possibility to actually happen neutralized his fear. Sure, he might fumble over a phrase or forget a reference or a quote, but if he did, he was prepared to ask his audience for help. By approaching his presentation based on what he knew he could do, it eliminated his fear about what he would never do.

The result? A natural, flowing rhetoric that seemed spontaneous and appropriate for the occasion and the crowd.

If you feel like you're on the point of losing it (passing out, throwing up, or freezing) and you're already behind the podium and/or in front of your audience, tell them *how excited you are to be there, and you're really looking forward to hearing their feedback after you finish.*

Use these exact words and notice what happens. Most beginning speakers experience an immediate change in physical state, allowing them to move forward and continue with their presentation.

If possible, meet members of the audience beforehand. That way, you're not speaking to a room full of strangers. Just before you move to the front of the room or take the stage, try to locate where they're sitting and direct the initial part of your presentation to them, as if they are the only ones you're speaking to.

Finally, don't even think about using alcohol or drugs to "take the edge off." There are plenty who've done it and they end up regretting it. It's like trying to get maximum performance out of a sports car after poking holes in the tires.

.

www.ingramcontent.com/pod-product-compliance
Lightning Source LLC
Chambersburg PA
CBHW060543200326
41521CB00007B/459